Nguyen-Thinh Le

Using Weighted Constraints To Build Tutoring Systems

Nguyen-Thinh Le

Using Weighted Constraints To Build Tutoring Systems

A Study Case in Logic Programming

Südwestdeutscher Verlag für Hochschulschriften

Impressum/Imprint (nur für Deutschland/only for Germany)
Bibliografische Information der Deutschen Nationalbibliothek: Die Deutsche Nationalbibliothek verzeichnet diese Publikation in der Deutschen Nationalbibliografie; detaillierte bibliografische Daten sind im Internet über http://dnb.d-nb.de abrufbar.
Alle in diesem Buch genannten Marken und Produktnamen unterliegen warenzeichen-, marken- oder patentrechtlichem Schutz bzw. sind Warenzeichen oder eingetragene Warenzeichen der jeweiligen Inhaber. Die Wiedergabe von Marken, Produktnamen, Gebrauchsnamen, Handelsnamen, Warenbezeichnungen u.s.w. in diesem Werk berechtigt auch ohne besondere Kennzeichnung nicht zu der Annahme, dass solche Namen im Sinne der Warenzeichen- und Markenschutzgesetzgebung als frei zu betrachten wären und daher von jedermann benutzt werden dürften.

Coverbild: www.ingimage.com

Verlag: Südwestdeutscher Verlag für Hochschulschriften GmbH & Co. KG
Heinrich-Böcking-Str. 6-8, 66121 Saarbrücken, Deutschland
Telefon +49 681 37 20 271-1, Telefax +49 681 37 20 271-0
Email: info@svh-verlag.de

Approved by: Hamburg, Universität, Diss., 2011

Herstellung in Deutschland (siehe letzte Seite)
ISBN: 978-3-8381-3263-1

Imprint (only for USA, GB)
Bibliographic information published by the Deutsche Nationalbibliothek: The Deutsche Nationalbibliothek lists this publication in the Deutsche Nationalbibliografie; detailed bibliographic data are available in the Internet at http://dnb.d-nb.de.
Any brand names and product names mentioned in this book are subject to trademark, brand or patent protection and are trademarks or registered trademarks of their respective holders. The use of brand names, product names, common names, trade names, product descriptions etc. even without a particular marking in this works is in no way to be construed to mean that such names may be regarded as unrestricted in respect of trademark and brand protection legislation and could thus be used by anyone.

Cover image: www.ingimage.com

Publisher: Südwestdeutscher Verlag für Hochschulschriften GmbH & Co. KG
Heinrich-Böcking-Str. 6-8, 66121 Saarbrücken, Germany
Phone +49 681 37 20 271-1, Fax +49 681 37 20 271-0
Email: info@svh-verlag.de

Printed in the U.S.A.
Printed in the U.K. by (see last page)
ISBN: 978-3-8381-3263-1

Copyright © 2012 by the author and Südwestdeutscher Verlag für Hochschulschriften GmbH & Co. KG and licensors
All rights reserved. Saarbrücken 2012

Acknowledgement

Special thanks to my principal supervisor Prof. Wolfgang Menzel for his conscientious guidance which more or less impacts on my way of life. Many thanks to my supervisor Prof. Niels Pinkwart from Clausthal University of Technology, who advised me of preparing empirical evaluations and gave valuable feedback on this thesis.

I would like to thank the members of the Natural Language System group, especially Solomon Teferra Abate, Thomas Kopinski and Lidia Khmylko, for helping me conduct system evaluations. I appreciate the library staff and Reinhard Zierke from the computer lab of the Department of Informatics for their constant help.

Finally, I am grateful to my family, in particular my little son, for presenting me a happy home after work and to my spiritual teacher Thich Nhat Hanh for showing me the beauty of the present moment.

Zusammenfassung

Programmierprobleme stellen eine große Herausforderung für die Entwicklung eines Tutorensystems dar, weil sie auf viele verschiedenen Art und Weise gelöst werden können. Um dem Studenten beim Lösen eines Programmierproblems effektiv helfen zu können, muss das Tutorensystem einen großen Raum von möglichen Lösungen abdecken und die Ursache eines Fehlers identifizieren können, wenn eine Lösung fehlerhaft ist. Die constraint-basierte Technik ist einer der viel versprechenden Ansätze zur Modellierung von Wissen für Tutorensysteme. Das Ziel dieser Arbeit ist, die Verwendbarkeit dieses Ansatzes in der Domäne der Programmierung zu untersuchen. Dabei fokussiert die Arbeit auf Logikprogrammierung.

Diese Arbeit stellt ein zweistufiges Tutorenmodell vor: Analysieren einer Aufgabenstellung vor der Implementierung. Für beide Schritte wird der Lösungsraum auf der Grundlage von *Constraints* im Zusammenspiel mit einer *Semantiktabelle* mo-delliert. Die Semantiktabelle dient dazu, die semantischen Anforderungen einer spe-zifischen Aufgabe zu repräsentieren. Außerdem wird von Transformationsregeln Gebrauch gemacht, um die Abdeckung des Lösungsraums zu vergrößern. Um hochwertige Rückmeldungen zu einer Studentenlösung liefern zu können, müssen Hypothesen über die Lösungsvariante des Studenten hinsichtlich ihrer Plausibilität bewertet werden. Zu diesem Zweck schlägt diese Arbeit vor, jedes Constraint mit einem *Gewicht* zu erweitern. Constraint-Gewichte werden eingesetzt, 1) um das Fehlerdiagnoseverfahren zu steuern; 2) um eine Entscheidung für die plausibelste Hypothese über die Intention des Studenten im Hinblick auf die implementierte Lösungsstrategie zu treffen; und 3) um Prioritäten für die Fehlernachrichten zu setzen. Mit Hilfe von gewichteten Constraints und dem zweistufigen Tutorenmodell wurde ein Tutorensystem für die Logikprogrammierung entwickelt.

Im Rahmen einer Offline-Evaluation wurde es gezeigt, dass das System eine relative hohe Diagnosegenauigkeit erreichte. In 90,8% der Implementierungen konnte die Lösungsstrategie korrekt bestimmt werden, und in 92,7% dieser Fälle wurden auch die Fehler korrekt diagnostiziert. Eine Online-Evaluation mit Studenten einer Lehrveranstaltung zur Logikprogrammierung ergab, dass durch die Arbeit mit dem System eine Verbesserung der Fertigkeiten in der Logikprogrammierung mit einer Effektstärke von zwischen 0,23 und 0,33 Standardabweichungen erreicht werden konnte.

Abstract

Programming problems constitute a significant challenge for the development of tutoring systems, because they can be solved in many different ways. To help the student solve a programming problem effectively, the tutoring system must be able to cover a large space of possible solutions. If a student solution has shortcomings, the system must be able to identify the reason why that solution is not correct. In the state of the art, one of the most promising approaches to modelling knowledge for tutoring systems is the constraint-based technique. This approach uses constraints to model a space of correct solutions, rather than enumerating them. The goal of this thesis is to investigate the applicability of this approach to develop tutoring systems for programming with the focus on logic programming.

This thesis presents a two-stage coaching strategy as a tutoring model which is intended to support the student in analysing a programming task prior to the implementation itself. For both coaching stages, the solution space is modelled on the basis of *constraints* in combination with a *semantic table* which is used to represent semantic requirements for a specific programming problem. In addition, transformation rules are used to extend the space of possible implementations. To be able to provide qualitative feedback on the student solution, hypotheses about the student's solution variant need to be evaluated with respect to their plausibility. For this purpose, this thesis proposes to enrich each constraint with a *weight* value indicating the importance of that constraint. Constraint weights serve three purposes. They are used to 1) control the process of error diagnosis, 2) to hypothesize the student's intention in terms of the implemented solution strategy, and 3) to prioritize feedback messages according to the severity of diagnosed errors.

To explore the capability of weighted constraints and the usefulness of the two-stage coaching model, a web-based tutoring system for logic programming has been implemented. Two evaluation studies have been conducted for this system. The first one showed that the system achieves a high diagnostic accuracy. In 90.8% of the student implementations the solution strategy could be hypothesized correctly and in 92.7% of cases, in which the solution strategy could be determined, errors were diagnosed correctly. The second study provided the evidence that the system did contribute to the improvement of the students' programming skills. The students who used the system outperformed their peers of the control group by an effect size between 0.23 and 0.33 standard deviations.

Contents

Acknowledgement   i

Zusammenfassung   iii

Abstract   v

1 Introduction   **1**
    1.1 Motivation 1
    1.2 Tutoring Systems 2
    1.3 The Problem of Error Diagnosis 3
    1.4 The Approach 6
    1.5 Research Goal and Hypotheses 10
    1.6 Overview 11

2 Tutoring Programming   **13**
    2.1 Tutoring By Coaching 13
    2.2 Programming 13
       2.2.1 Programming Phases 13
       2.2.2 Knowledge Required for Programming 15
    2.3 Two Levels of Solution Variability 16
       2.3.1 Solution Strategy 16
       2.3.2 Implementation 18
    2.4 Classification of Problems 19
    2.5 Tutoring Systems for Programming 20
    2.6 Approaches to Error Diagnosis 25
       2.6.1 Library of Plans and Bugs 26
       2.6.2 Program Transformation 28
       2.6.3 Model-Tracing 30

	2.6.4	Constraint-based Modelling	33
	2.6.5	A Summary of The State of The Art	38

3 A Coaching System For Logic Programming — 41

- 3.1 Logic Programming - A Case Study 42
  - 3.1.1 Simplified Prolog 42
  - 3.1.2 Solution Space 43
  - 3.1.3 High Level Programming Knowledge 49
- 3.2 Requirements 51
- 3.3 Conceptual Design 52
- 3.4 A Two-Stage Coaching Model 53
  - 3.4.1 A Preliminary Study 53
  - 3.4.2 Task Analysis 57
  - 3.4.3 Implementation 59
- 3.5 Modelling Programming Knowledge 60
  - 3.5.1 A Constraint-based Model 60
  - 3.5.2 A Formalism For Weighted Constraints 62
- 3.6 Modelling The Space of Predicate Signatures 65
- 3.7 Modelling The Space of Implementations 67
  - 3.7.1 An Implementation Table 67
  - 3.7.2 Weighted Constraints 69
  - 3.7.3 Transformation Rules 74
- 3.8 Error Diagnosis 75
  - 3.8.1 Hypothesis Generation 76
  - 3.8.2 Hypothesis Evaluation 78
  - 3.8.3 Signature Diagnosis 78
  - 3.8.4 Implementation Diagnosis 80
- 3.9 Feedback 88
  - 3.9.1 Feedback Messages 90
  - 3.9.2 Ranking and Grouping Feedback Messages 91
  - 3.9.3 Error Location 91
- 3.10 Limitations 92

4 Implementation — 93

- 4.1 Architecture 93

		4.2	User Interface	94
		4.3	Back-End Components	95
		4.4	Knowledge Base	97

5 Evaluation 99
    5.1 Goals . . . 99
    5.2 Diagnostic Accuracy . . . 100
        5.2.1 Intention Analysis . . . 101
        5.2.2 Diagnostic Validity . . . 102
        5.2.3 Related Work and Discussion . . . 104
    5.3 Learning Effect . . . 106
        5.3.1 Design . . . 106
        5.3.2 Results . . . 107
        5.3.3 Related Work and Discussion . . . 110

6 Conclusions 115
    6.1 Summary . . . 115
    6.2 Thesis Contributions . . . 118
    6.3 Future Research . . . 120

A Test A 125
    A.1 Original Version . . . 125
    A.2 English Version . . . 126

B Tutorial 128
    B.1 Original Version . . . 128
    B.2 English Version . . . 128

C Experiment Exercises 131
    C.1 Original Version . . . 131
    C.2 English Version . . . 132

D Test B 133
    D.1 Original Version . . . 133
    D.2 English version . . . 134

E Questionnaire 135

E.1	Original version	135
E.2	English version	136

F A Programming Task: Calculate salaries   **137**

G A Sample Student Solution   **138**
    G.1 Example 1 138
    G.2 Example 2 139

Bibliography   **141**

Index   **151**

List of Tables

1.1	Implementation of four solution strategies for the problem *Investment*	5
2.1	Knowledge required for different phases of programming	15
2.2	A classification of tutoring systems for programming	23
2.3	Program analysers	25
2.4	Plans and bugs-based vs. program transformation-based approach	38
2.5	Model-tracing vs. constraint-based approach	39
3.1	Error rate in the programming phases	54
3.2	A signature table for the problem *Investment*	66
3.3	An implementation table for the problem *Investment*	69
3.4	Used constraint weights	74
3.5	Modelling techniques	75
3.6	Time consumption and diagnostic accuracy	82
3.7	Plausibility of hypotheses about the implemented solution strategy	89
4.1	Number of constraints	97
5.1	Evaluation of the intention analysis	101
5.2	Categories for Precision and Recall	103
5.3	Evaluation of the diagnostic validity	104
5.4	A comparison of the diagnostic accuracy	105
5.5	Number of experiment participants	106
5.6	Learning gains	108
5.7	The effect size Cohen's d	108
5.8	Free comments provided by the experimental group	111
5.9	Learning benefits of different tutoring systems for programming	111
5.10	Percentage of not fixed errors	112

List of Figures

1.1 Implementation variants of the tail recursive strategy. 6
1.2 A solution space determined by the constraints 7

2.1 An iterative process of programming 14
2.2 A sample task in geometry. 17
2.3 A definition for the goal Sentinel-Controlled-Input in PROUST. 26
2.4 A plan for implementing the goal Sentinel-Controlled-Input in PROUST. 27
2.5 Two different transformation models 29

3.1 The structural hierarchy of a Prolog predicate. 43
3.2 A small hierarchy of Prolog patterns. 51
3.3 The structural hierarchy of a predicate signature. 65
3.4 The generation of hypotheses about a student implementation 86

4.1 The architecture of INCOM 94
4.2 The user interface for task analysis. 95
4.3 The user interface for implementation. 96

5.1 Participants' ratings on the precision of error location and the expressiveness of feedback messages 109
5.2 Participants' ratings on the user interface and the tutoring model 110
5.3 Participants' ratings on their motivation and their transferability 110
5.4 Participants' ratings on the helpfulness and the deployment of the system 111

6.1 Compressible diagnostic results 120

B.1 A tutorial for the first coaching stage: task analysis 129
B.2 A tutorial for the second coaching stage: implementation. 130

Chapter 1

Introduction

1.1 Motivation

Recently, a study commissioned by the Bertelsmann foundation showed that in Germany almost 1.1 million school students require private tuition (*"Nachhilfe"* in German) regularly, and for this purpose around 950 million to 1.5 billion Euro are being spent every year (Klemm and Klemm, 2010). The authors of the study also point out that private tuition has benefits for the learning performance of students. However, private tuition is expensive. Not all parents can afford this kind of learning support for their children. This impairs the equality of opportunity of the education system. A possible solution to this problem is to provide students with information technology enabled learning tools after school, thus reducing the demand for private tuition. Several studies have reported on the effectiveness of deploying information technology in education (Regian, 1997; Kadiyala and Crynes, 1998).

Programming courses constitute an indispensable part of the study of informatics because programming knowledge, either imperative, object-oriented, or functional, is the prerequisite for other courses of this study. A computer programming course may take place in many forms: e.g., lecture, homework and practical session or a combination of them. In spite of the substantial effort involved in teaching, learning to program is challenging for many beginners and the acquisition of programming skills is difficult. Soloway et al. (1982) and McCracken et al. (2001) have shown that students still have a lack of programming competence after a full year of programming instruction.

The motivation of this thesis is to discuss how information technology can be used to relieve the difficulties of programming learners and to help them improve their programming skills.

1.2 Tutoring Systems

The application of information technology in education goes back to the beginning of the 20th century when Pressey (1927) built a machine providing multiple-choice questions for learners. From the early 1960s, educational researchers and training developers used computers to solve their practical problems, e.g., creating electronic course books, and *computer-aided instruction* (CAI) systems began to take shape. The learning principle underlying CAI systems was based on the behaviouristic theory which assumes that learning is a process of memorizing, demonstrating, and imitating (Skinner, 1958). Based on this principle, learning strategies targeted primarily at memory tasks and recall. Thus, drill exercises aimed at testing whether the students had acquired sufficient knowledge so far and how to reinforce the required knowledge (Suppes et al., 1968).

Since the CAI systems were too rigid and could not provide learning material to the students individually, in the mid 1970s, they were improved to be adaptive, i.e., curriculum lessons, exercises and feedback were provided according to the current knowledge of each student. Such systems were referred to as *adaptive computer-aided instruction* systems.

Adaptive computer-aided instruction systems became *Intelligent Tutoring Systems* (ITS), when researchers changed their focus on two aspects. First, the learning principle was shifted from learning-by-memorizing to learning-by-problem-solving which corresponds to the constructivist learning theory (Dewey, 1910; Sleeman and Brown, 1982). According to this theory, students construct new knowledge from their own experience, and they are required to engage actively in the learning process. Thus, developers of ITS emphasized on providing compelling practical exercises to the students rather than offering only course books and drill exercises. Second, ITS are more "intelligent" than adaptive CAI systems because ITS are able to diagnose errors in student solutions, make assumptions about the student's current knowledge, and adapt instruction according to the student's need (Shute and Psotka, 1996, p. 576). These abilities are derived from the underlying models of the system. Typically, an intelligent tutoring system contains four types of knowledge: a domain model, a student model, a tutoring model, and a communication model (Woolf, 2009).

A domain model represents knowledge about the domain being tutored. This type of knowledge may include facts, definitions, and problem solving algorithms of a domain and serves two purposes: 1) diagnosing errors in student solutions, and 2) presenting new lessons or new problems (which can be hard-coded or dynamically generated). A student model is the representation of information about the state of knowledge (including correct knowledge and misconceptions) of each student (or a group of students). The student model serves to plan and control the interaction with the student: e.g., selecting an appropriate problem/lesson or modulating feedback messages. Commonly, results from diagnosing errors in student solutions (e.g., misconceptions, time spent on problems, requested corrective hints, correct answers) are the most important source of information which can be used to make assumptions about the student's performance of the domain being learned. Additionally, information about learning styles, affective state (boring, interesting), or the learning pace of the student can also be used to improve the quality of the student model. A tutoring model encapsulates the pedagogical expertise which is used to decide on a pedagogical action (e.g., choose next lesson or problem for presenting), and includes methods for reasoning about feedback messages. The communication model is required to manage the communication between the student and the tutoring system. A typical intelligent tutoring system exploits the four types of knowledge in a cyclic way. First, the system uses domain knowledge to select customized problems/lessons for presentation to the student and diagnosis of errors in the student solutions. Then, the system reasons about the student's current knowledge state and updates the student model. Finally, the system applies tutoring and communication knowledge to select appropriate feedback and to choose the style of presentation.

In reality, the demarcation between ITS and CAI systems is not always clear because many CAI systems also exhibit one or more "intelligent features" of ITS (Wenger, 1987). Thus, in this thesis, all types of computer-aided systems (CAI, adaptive CAI, and ITS) are referred to as *tutoring systems*. Whether a tutoring system is intelligent or not, this depends on how much "intelligence" has been implemented in it.

1.3 The Problem of Error Diagnosis

Error diagnosis plays a key role in an intelligent tutoring system. Diagnostic information which is obtained from diagnosing errors in student solutions serves to form and upgrade the student model - the component which enables the adaptivity of a tutoring system. A faithful student model needs to be updated dynamically because the student can make improvement during the learning process. Thus, diagnostic information must be accurate and plausible. This requires an adequate domain model which is able to cover the space of all possible solutions for a given problem and a mechanism to derive the reason why an erroneous solution does not belong to that space.

For a problem in the domain of programming, the solution space can be very large because there are alternative solution strategies to be applied. A solution strategy is a way to solve a class of frequently occurring problem situations. According to Pennington and Grabowski

(1990); Weiser and Shertz (1983); Hoc (1988), expert programmers have several solution strategies at hand after the characteristics of a given problem have been identified. The concept of solution strategy will be discussed in more details in Section 2.3. In addition to the number of possible solution strategies for a given programming problem, each of them can be implemented in many variants using different programming constructs. Therefore, in order to give high quality feedback on errors occurring in a solution, it is necessary to build a hypothesis about the student's solution variant, then identify and explain errors based on that hypothesis. Otherwise, diagnostic information will not be useful because it can be confusing to the student. The first question a tutoring system for programming needs to answer is: *Which solution strategy did the programmer choose?*

The problem of error diagnosis in a program can be illustrated using the sample task *Investment*: "Write a predicate/function to compute the return after investing an amount of money at a constant yearly interest rate". To solve this problem, the following strategies can be applied:

1. *Analytic strategy*: The profit of investing a sum of money *Sum* with a yearly interest *Rate* after a *Period* of years is calculated based on a mathematical geometric series like `Sum*(Rate+1)^Period`.

2. *Tail recursive strategy*: A variable can be used to accumulate the sum of investing money and its interest after each year.

3. *Recursive and arithmetic_before strategy*: The calculation of the profit of investing a sum of money goes back year after year to the first year of investment, then the return of each year is determined by summing up the investing money and its interest.

4. *Recursive and arithmetic_after strategy*: The return is calculated recursively on a new period, then the new period is checked whether the old period is an increment of the new one. Following this strategy, a new period is not calculated, rather tested.

To answer the question above, the most plausible hypothesis about the student's intention of choosing the solution strategy needs to be decided in order to provide appropriate feedback.

The solution space of a programming problem not only is determined by the number of possible solution strategies, but also by the number of alternative implementation variants. Each of the solution strategies for the problem *Investment* can be implemented in many ways. Thus, to diagnose errors in a student solution, a tutoring system needs to answer the second question: *How did the programmer implement the chosen solution strategy?*

1.3. THE PROBLEM OF ERROR DIAGNOSIS

To investigate the problem of error diagnosis in a tutoring system for programming, this thesis takes logic programming as a study case due to two reasons. First, the dual semantics of this programming paradigm is an attractive feature: a logic program[1] can be interpreted either declaratively or procedurally (Brna, 2001). Thus, the techniques which are used to model the procedural elements of a logic program can be learned and may be partly transferred to procedural languages. Second, since a logic programming language can be understood as the relational calculus enriched with recursion and function symbols, the techniques used to diagnose logic programs may also be applied to the paradigm of declarative programming in general.

Table 1.1: Implementation of four solution strategies for the problem *Investment*

Analytic	Tail recursive	Rec_arith_before	Rec_arith_after
inv(S,R,P,Ret):- Ret is S*(R+1)^P.	inv(S,_,P,Ret):- P=0, S=Ret. inv(S,R,P,Ret):- P>0, NS is S*R+S, NP is P-1, inv(NS,R,NP,Ret).	inv(S,_,P,Ret):- P=0, S=Ret. inv(S,R,P,Ret):- $P > 0$, NP is P-1, inv(S,R,NP,NS), Ret is NS + R*NS.	inv(S,_,P,Ret):- P=0, S=Ret. inv(S,R,P,Ret):- inv(S, R, NP, NS), P is NP +1, Ret is NS+R*NS.

Table 1.1 shows the implementation of those four solution strategies in a normal form in Prolog (cf. Section 3.7.1), where the four argument positions of the predicate *inv* represent start money, yearly interest rate, period of investment, and return. For each solution strategy, many semantic-preserving variants can be implemented. For instance, the *tail recursive* strategy can be implemented in many ways by varying the order of the two clauses or the order of the second and the third subgoal of the second clause, choosing one of two unification techniques (implicit and explicit), or using the commutative and distributive laws in mathematics to transform arithmetic expressions as illustrated in Figure 1.1. In total, there might exist several thousands of correct implementations for the problem *Investment*. If helper predicates are deployed to modularize a code, the solution space for this problem becomes open-ended, because defining helper predicates is beyond the scope of any anticipation. Thus, a hypothesis about the intention of the student choosing an implementation variant is also required to provide an appropriate corrective hint.

For instance, we assume that a student has intended to implement the tail recursive strategy.

---

[1] We use the term *"program"* only when discussing about the specific domain of programming. In general cases, we use the term *"solution"*. A program which is created by the student is then referred to as *student program*.

However, she[2] has implemented a wrong guard which should check whether the investment period is positive like P>=0 (compare with the second column of Table 1.1). Trying to answer the second question means in this case to hypothesize whether she intended to implement the guard like (X>0) or (X>=1). For the former, we can suggest to correct the error by changing the operator to X>0, and for the latter the operand on the right hand side should be corrected to value 1. Hypothesizing a student's intention is meant to answer the two questions above: *which solution strategy did she choose and how did she implement that solution strategy?*

The problem being addressed in this thesis is therefore how to model a large solution space for a programming problem provided by a tutoring system for logic programming and how to diagnose errors in the student programs accurately in accordance with the student's intention.

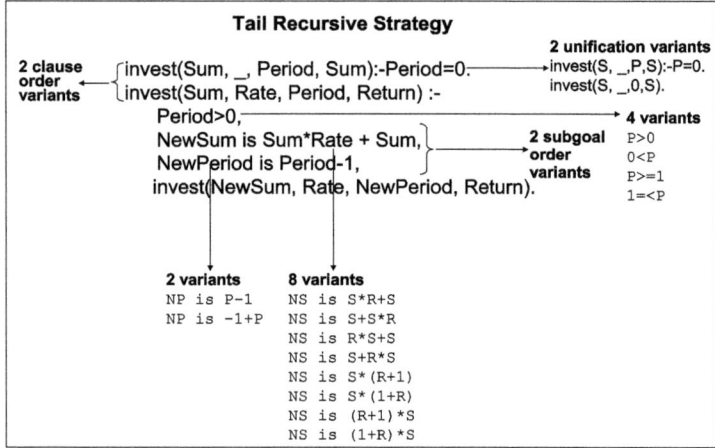

Figure 1.1: Implementation variants of the tail recursive strategy.

1.4 The Approach

Over the last two decades, numerous approaches to error diagnosis in the domain of programming have been devised, such as the plan and bug library-based (Johnson, 1990; Looi, 1991; Weber and Brusilovsky, 2001), program transformation-based (Gegg-Harrison, 1993; Vanneste, 1994; Hong, 2004), model tracing (Anderson and Reiser, 1985) and constraint-based modelling (CBM) techniques (Ohlsson, 1994; Ohlsson and Mitrovic, 2006). Among these, cognitive learning theories underlie the model tracing and CBM approaches which have been applied

---

[2] For the sake of brevity, we use "she", "herself", "her", ect., generally to refer to both genders.

1.4. THE APPROACH

successfully to build tutoring systems.

In a model-tracing tutoring system, domain knowledge is represented by an expert model and a library of *buggy rules*. The expert model represents one or more *"ideal"* solution paths to a given problem, and buggy rules[3] anticipate possible erroneous problem solving steps of the student. Error diagnosis and instruction are carried out by tracing every problem solving step of the student. Whenever the student solution deviates from the expert model, the system provides diagnostic information based on buggy rules. Model-tracing tutoring systems have proven to be successful in several domains, e.g., Physics (VanLehn et al., 2005) and Algebra (Heffernan et al., 2008).

Recently, the constraint-based modelling approach, which focuses on static cognitive states rather than problem solving processes, has been showing great promise as an alternative. A constraint represents a domain principle or specifies a property of correct solutions. A set of constraints divides the space of solutions into two subspaces: the inner space for correct[4] and the outer space for incorrect solutions as Figure 1.2 illustrates. Whenever a solution violates a constraint, that solution falls into the outer space, and a CBM tutoring system derives a feedback associated to that violated constraint.

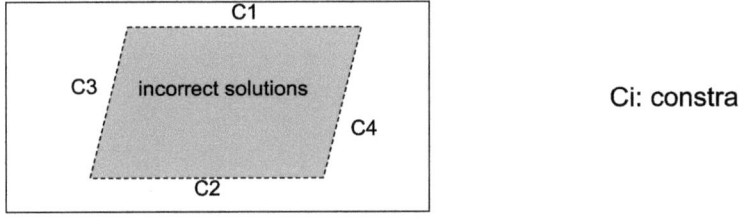

Figure 1.2: A solution space determined by the constraints

The CBM approach has been employed successfully to develop a SQL tutoring system (Mitrovic et al., 2001) and to diagnose grammatical errors in natural language utterances (Menzel, 1988). Researchers agree that this approach is promising due to the following factors:

- A separate expert model is not necessary because the expert information is encapsulated in the constraints (Ohlsson, 1994). Creating an expert model by modelling a large number of solution paths, e.g., several thousands of solutions, is a laborious undertaking compared to the task of collecting a limited set of domain principles and properties of correct solutions for a problem.

---

[3] *Buggy production* and *buggy rules* are the terminology in the literature of model-tracing tutors.
[4] From now, if not explicitly discussing about incorrect solutions, the term "solutions" indicates correct solutions.

- A constraint-based system does not require anticipating erroneous behaviours of students.

- The constraint-based approach is more tolerant than the model tracing one with regards to the incompleteness of the knowledge base. A model-tracing system flags a correct solution as erroneous if it does not meet the problem solving steps specified in the expert model, whereas in a constraint-based system, an erroneous solution is still considered being correct as long as no constraint is violated (Mitrovic and Ohlsson, 1999).

In particular, with respect to the domain of programming, the constraint-based approach is superior to model-tracing due to two reasons. First, programming is an iterative process, i.e., the programmer develops a program by refining and revising it incrementally whereas the model-tracing approach tends to model a linear problem solving process: problem solving is viewed as a sequence of many steps. Model tracing approach can be applied in the domain of programming under assumption that the process of problem solving of the student can be observed and guided strictly by the tutoring system, for instance, the LISP-Tutor (Anderson and Reiser, 1985). Second, the constraint-based approach models a space of correct solutions while the model-tracing approach requires to enumerate each correct solution path and to anticipate a number of erroneous paths. Creating an expert model by modelling a number of solution paths, e.g., several thousands solutions, is a laborious undertaking compared to the task of collecting a small set of principles of a programming language and properties of correct solutions. Thus, the constraint-based approach is applicable to build an exploratory learning environment which encourages students to create their own solutions to problems creatively (Gutierrez-Santos and Mavrikis, 2008). Therefore, this thesis adopts CBM as the basic approach to diagnosing errors in logic programs.

However, the constraint-based approach comes with several weaknesses with respect to error diagnosis. First, this approach is not able to evaluate the plausibility of hypotheses about different solution variants for a problem. Constraints might be satisfied under the assumption of one solution strategy, but could be violated in the context of another strategy. If the dependence between constraints and a specific solution strategy is not explicitly modelled, diagnostic information which is derived from a violated constraint might be deceptive to the student, because the solution strategy the student intended to implement might not agree with the one based on which constraints are checked. Therefore, this problem raises the need to enhance the constraint-based error diagnosis with the capability of hypothesizing the student's intention.

In order to choose the most plausible hypothesis, approaches to softening constraints in

1.4. THE APPROACH

constraint satisfaction problems (CSPs) can be exploited. The most popular frameworks considering soft constraints include fuzzy CSPs (Dubois et al., 1996), partial CSPs (Freuder and Wallace, 1992), cost-minimizing CSPs[5](Schiex et al., 1995), and probabilistic CSPs (Fargier and Lang, 1993). Among these, this thesis proposes to adopt the probabilistic CSPs approach because it does not evaluate a constraint system partially (like the partial CSPs framework) and nor is it necessary to specify constraints with possible instantiations of constraint variables in advance (like fuzzy and cost-minimizing CSPs frameworks). The probabilistic CSPs approach requires that each constraint is associated with a probability indicating the importance level of that constraint. This approach has been applied successfully to enhance the quality of error diagnosis, e.g., for natural language sentences (Menzel and Schröder, 1998), or to diagnose the shortcomings of intermediate hypotheses of a natural language parser with the goal to guide the system towards an optimal parsing result (Foth, 2007). Following the probabilistic CSPs approach, we enrich constraints with heuristic information referred to as *constraint weight* which indicates the importance of each constraint. We use constraint weights to serve three essential purposes: 1) to control the process of error diagnosis, 2) to decide on the most plausible hypothesis about the strategy underlying a student solution, and 3) to prioritize feedback messages according to the importance of each diagnostic information. The first and the second purpose can be achieved by generating and evaluating hypotheses about the solution strategy and the implementation variant of the student. The third purpose can be realised using the weight values of violated constraints to distinguish the severity of each error.

The second weakness of the constraint-based approach is the incoherence of feedback messages which are derived from violated constraints. Individual constraints encode domain principles which represent pieces of domain knowledge. But, the domain principles are not always orthogonal. Hence, feedback messages which are derived from these constraints are not related to each other. As a result, unrelated feedback messages are returned to the student, and this may lead to potential confusion of the student (Kodaganallur et al., 2005). Thus, a means to bind the feedback messages together is required. In the course of applying constraints to create the domain model, this thesis proposes to model standard solution strategies which are noted as *patterns*. Similar notions can be found in the object-oriented programming paradigm (Gamma et al., 1995). Constraints modelling patterns are referred to as *pattern constraints*. Since violated pattern constraints flag errors in the context of a standard solution strategy, pattern-related feedback messages can be presented in a coherent manner.

---

[5]In the literature, researchers refer to this kind of problems as *weighted* constraint satisfaction problems. We avoid to use this notion because we will use the term *weighted constraint* to describe the importance of a constraint later.

In order to diagnose the semantic correctness[6] of a student solution, it is necessary to model semantic properties for each solution strategy for a given programming problem. In principle, constraints alone can be used to model the semantic properties as Ohlsson proposed (Ohlsson, 1994). However, these constraints would be very complex and problem-specific. Every time a new problem needs to be integrated into a CBM system, it is necessary to specify new problem-specific constraints. This is not an easy task for problem authors who are not familiar with the constraint representation. Instead, Mitrovic et al. (2007) suggested to use an ideal solution to encapsulate the semantic information required for each problem. However, identifying an ideal solution within a large solution space for a programming problem is not an easy task. Furthermore, an ideal solution represents a single solution strategy while there may exist alternative solution strategies to solve a programming problem. Therefore, this thesis suggests to define a *semantic table* which represents the semantic information required by each possible solution strategy. The concept of using the semantic table comprises of two ideas: 1) modelling alternative solution strategies and 2) modelling generalised implementations.

In addition, this thesis focuses on the following issues which have not (or very little) been addressed in existing tutoring systems for programming: 1) coaching the students during the phase of the task analysis in addition to the implementation phase, 2) communicating with the students using both basic and high level programming concepts, and 3) supporting a free exploration of solutions to a programming problem. To address these issues, this thesis proposes a *two-stage coaching* strategy which requests the student to analyse the programming task prior to the implementation. The results of the task analysis are specified in form of a predicate signature to be implemented. Using the information of the specified predicate signature, the diagnosis process is able to derive some cues about the intention of the student, namely the purpose of each argument position. For implementing a solution, a free form user interface is provided. On each coaching stage, feedback messages are formulated in terms of basic and high level knowledge.

1.5 Research Goal and Hypotheses

Programming is a complex domain. A programming problem can be solved by alternative solution strategies and implemented in different ways. The goal of this thesis is to explore the potential and the limitations of the CBM technique with respect to developing tutoring systems for programming, where logic programming is focused and taken as a study case. This thesis proposes, and experimentally evaluates the following hypotheses:

---

[6]The meaning of a program is considered as its semantics. A programmer who can write a program in some programming language has at least an informal understanding of what that program means.

- **Hypothesis 1**: It is possible to build a domain model that covers a large solution space for a logic programming problem using the representation of weighted constraints, semantic tables, and a set of transformation rules.

- **Hypothesis 2**: Using the representations defined in Hypothesis 1, it is possible to develop an algorithm to diagnose errors in a logic program and to hypothesize the solution strategy correctly.

- **Hypothesis 3**: Using constraint weights, it is possible to prioritize diagnostic information according to the importance of errors.

- **Hypothesis 4**: It is possible to create a knowledge base of standard solution strategies in logic programming using weighted constraints and to group feedback messages in a coherent manner.

- **Hypothesis 5**: A tutoring system for logic programming, which is developed on the basis of weighted constraints, semantic tables, a set of transformation rules, and the two-stage coaching model, is able to help students improve their skills in solving logic programming problems.

1.6 Overview

The remainder of the dissertation is structured as follows:

Chapter 2 introduces tutoring by coaching which, we argue, is capable of helping students solve programming problems. Relevant characteristics of the domain of programming are identified: the phases of the programming process and the required programming knowledge, the factors which determine the solution space of a programming problem. Existing tutoring systems for programming are reviewed and classified based on these characteristics to give us a picture of their capability. Finally, this chapter reviews existing approaches to error diagnosis, discusses the applicability of the constraint-based approach in the domain of programming and the weaknesses which need to be addressed.

Chapter 3 is in many ways the center piece of the dissertation. It presents the tutoring model and the domain model for a tutoring system which is intended to help students solve problems in logic programming. As a tutoring model, the chapter proposes a two-stage coaching strategy: the task analysis prior to the implementation. The chapter also presents how to model the solution space for a logic programming problem using weighted constraints, semantic tables, and transformation rules. Finally, this chapter demonstrates how error diagnosis can be carried out based on this domain model.

Chapter 4 illustrates a tutoring system for logic programming (INCOM) which has been implemented according to the proposals presented in Chapter 3. The chapter describes the architecture of the system.

Chapter 5 reports two evaluation studies. The first one aims at evaluating the quality of diagnostic results provided by the system. The goal of the second one is to investigate the effectiveness of the system with respect to improving the programming skills of students. The evaluation studies show that the tutoring system INCOM, which is built on the basis of weighted constraints, semantic tables, transformation rules, and the two-stage coaching model, provides fairly accurate diagnostic information compared to other existing tutoring systems for programming, and students who used the system to solve logic programming problems did outperform the participants of the control group.

The dissertation concludes with Chapter 6. It summarizes the general arguments of the dissertation, discusses the main findings, reviews the main contributions, and proposes future work.

Chapter 2

Tutoring Programming

2.1 Tutoring By Coaching

Programming is a domain in which not only the ability to reproduce knowledge, but also the skill to solve problems is the focus of attention of the instruction. Therefore, tutoring programming should promote learning by doing. Like classroom instruction, tutoring can be performed in many forms, one of which is coaching the student solving problems. Brown et al. (1989) defined coaching as "the learning support aimed at improving the performance of a student during the carrying out of a task". This way, the tutor helps the student to overcome impasses along the process of problem solving by providing targeted feedback or solution hints (VanLehn et al., 2003; Merrill et al., 1992). The goal of coaching is to bring the performance of the student closer to that of an expert (Collins et al., 1989).

2.2 Programming

2.2.1 Programming Phases

Researchers agree that the *process of programming* can be divided into four phases (Pennington and Grabowski, 1990; Feddon and Charness, 1999):

1. *Task analysis*: In this phase, the programmer tries to understand the problem. To achieve this, she needs to have enough knowledge in the problem domain, e.g., basic knowledge in finance is required to calculate the compound interest of investment. The result of problem understanding is a mental conception of the problem which should be documented in an appropriate form (e.g., a list of parameters which represent information and goals in the problem description).

2. *Design*: The programmer decomposes the given problem and produces the description

of the program in an intermediate representation (e.g., schema-like code, diagrams, or a modelling language like UML).

3. *Implementation*: The programmer converts the designed solution into program code of a specific programming language.

4. *Validation*: The programmer tests whether the program fulfils the requirements specified in the problem description. In the negative case, the program needs to be debugged and repaired.

In practice, expert programmers do not follow these phases strictly, and rarely complete one task before moving on to the next phase. Rather, they interweave work on various phases (Malhotra et al., 1980). However, Feddon and Charness (1999) recommended that programming beginners should not be allowed to practice programming like experienced programmers. Similarly to learning writing alphabetic characters by hand, beginners strictly have to follow the instructions of how to draw a character, whereas *"experienced"* people do not have to.

There are two views of how the process of programming should be carried out: linear or iterative (Larman and Basili, 2003). According to the first view, it can be seen as flowing steadily downwards through the phases, and this is called a waterfall model. However, this model has been criticized as being impractical because it is almost impossible to get one phase of a software product's life cycle perfectly finished (even for a trivial software project) before moving on to next phases.

The second view is represented, for instance, by the spiral development model, which combines elements of design and prototyping-in-stages. That is, the process of programming starts initially with a small portion of requirements and is executed through the required phases. The resulting prototype is extended incrementally according to new requirements. According to this view, the phases of a software development process can be re-visited iteratively many times.

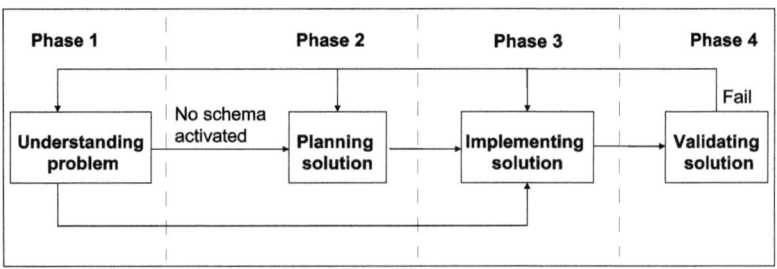

Figure 2.1: An iterative process of programming

2.2. PROGRAMMING

In reality, programmers (even experts) rarely produce a correct program on the first attempt. Thus, this thesis adopts the view that *programming is an iterative process*. This view corresponds to the process of solving a general problem (Figure 2.1) (Gick, 1986). In the first phase, the solver has to understand a given problem and mentally maps this information onto her prior knowledge of the problem domain.

In the second phase, a solution is designed and planned. If the solver is an expert, who possesses a rich amount of solution schemas (e.g., programming plans, programming techniques), which can be called *tacit knowledge* and have been built from the experience of solving a wide range of problems, she can skip this phase and starts to implement it. A beginner, however, tends to be less systematic (Pintrich et al., 1987). She does not have a suitable solution schema at hand, and thus, she has to search for a solution in a trial-and-error manner. Therefore, coaching a student solving programming problems should aim at transferring this kind of tacit knowledge to programming learners.

In the third phase, the designed solution is implemented by applying constructs of a formal language, e.g., a specific programming language. By entering the last phase, the solver validates the correctness of her implementation. If the implementation does not solve the given problem, the solver has to iterate through the implementation phase in order to detect wrong applications of the formal language. Alternatively, she can go back to the second phase to devise a new solution design, or to the task analysis phase to revise the knowledge required in the domain of the given problem.

2.2.2 Knowledge Required for Programming

What kind of knowledge should a programming learner acquire? To develop a program successfully, a programmer needs to have a range of different types of know-ledge which correspond to the phases of programming as Table 2.1 shows (Pennington and Grabowski, 1990). With respect to tutoring a programming language, we assume that the student has enough knowledge of a certain problem domain. With respect to tutoring beginners in programming normally two types of *programming knowledge* are focused: the programming language and algorithms.

Table 2.1: Knowledge required for different phases of programming

Phase	Knowledge Type
Task analysis	Domain knowledge (e.g., finance)
Design	Design strategies, algorithms, design language
Implementation	Programming language, programming conventions
Validation	All knowledge types, debugging, testing strategies

Shneiderman (1977) distinguished between *syntactic* and *semantic* knowledge of a programming language. Syntactic knowledge is constituted by the constructs of a programming language. Semantic knowledge is divided into *low* and *high* level. Low level knowledge represents the semantics of a programming construct. High level knowledge includes the semantics of stereotypic compositions of programming constructs which are used to solve particular programming problems. In summary, we distinguish three levels of programming knowledge.

- A *programming primitive* is a syntactic construct of a programming language.
- A *basic programming concept* is the semantic interpretation of a programming primitives. For example, several procedural languages, the operator "=" is used to assign a value to a variable, where in logic programming languages this operator has the meaning of unification.
- A *high level programming concept* is the semantic interpretation of a composition of several basic concepts. This type of knowledge is often conceived as *tacit knowledge* acquired by programming experts from their programming experience. In specific languages, researchers referred to instances of this type of programming knowledge as *schemas* (Rist, 1989), *programming clichés* (Waters, 1994), or *programming plans* (Johnson and Soloway, 1985). Recently, with the establishment of object-oriented programming languages like Java and C++, the gang of four (Gamma et al., 1995) proposed *design patterns* to represent tacit knowledge underlying object-oriented programs.

2.3 Two Levels of Solution Variability

2.3.1 Solution Strategy

Given a problem in a particular domain, an expert might have different solution strategies at her disposal (Le et al., 2010). Intuitively, a solution strategy is based on the available means which can be used to deal with frequently occurring problem situations. For instance, in the domain of travel planning, the task could consist in finding a route between two places. Depending on the available means of transportation different strategies can be applied: e.g., driving by car, taking a train, or taking a flight. In the domain of geometry, alternative solution strategies are based on the available theorems which have been proven. The task is to prove that the triangle ADE is isosceles given that angel <ABC is equal to angle <ACB (Figure 2.2), we either have to prove that DE is parallel to BC or that AD=AE holds.

Similarly, in the domain of programming, almost always different solution alternatives are available. In addition to different types of programming knowledge required for each phase of

2.3. TWO LEVELS OF SOLUTION VARIABILITY

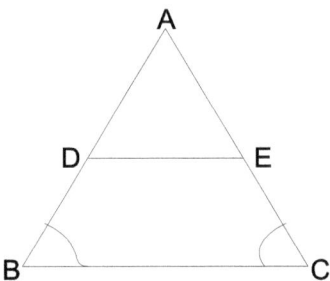

Figure 2.2: A sample task in geometry.

the process of programming, researchers suggested that expert programmers have some kinds of knowledge about problem categories and associated *solution strategies*[1] (Pennington and Grabowski, 1990; Weiser and Shertz, 1983; Hoc, 1988). That is, when a problem is given to an expert, she will identify its characteristics by associating it with previously solved problems and assign that problem to a solution strategy which might be applied to solve problems of that type. For instance, if the task is to write a function for the return on investment, four possible solution strategies can be applied (cf. Table 1.1). However, it is not always possible to determine a solution strategy immediately because most real-world programming problems are too complex to be assigned to a single category. Hoc (1988) suggested that the task of identifying the programming problem category and an appropriate solution strategy should take place in the design phase, where a complex programming problem can be decomposed into sub-problems for which solution strategies can be identified. The solution strategy for a complex programming problem can be built up from a combination of solution strategies applied to these sub-problems.

Pertaining to tutoring, identifying the strategy underlying a solution is an important issue. If feedback is meant to help the student improve her solution, it always has to be contextualized according to the solution strategy the student is obviously applying. Otherwise, it will not agree with the intention of the student and becomes useless or even confusing. This happens, for example, if the student has intended to implement the analytic strategy for the problem *Investment*, but the tutoring system returns corrective hints in the context of a normal recursive strategy.

In general, a solution strategy forms the basis for the process of finding a solution. However, it might be difficult to hypothesize the solution strategy from the solution itself if it contains

---

[1] The authors referred to a solution strategy as "problem solution plan".

too little information about the solution process as it is typical for simple arithmetic tasks. For example, in the domain of fractions, if a task is to find a correct number to replace the question mark for the equation: 12/15=?/5, a solution strategy can hardly be derived from a wrong answer. But if the solution to be provided by the student is richer in information (e.g., a travel plan, a proof, or a program), then there is a chance of inferring the solution strategy directly from the solution structure. In the domain of programming, for example, if the problem *Investment* is solved using Prolog, the implementation of the analytic solution strategy contains one clause executing an analytic formula, whereas the implementation of the tail recursive strategy contains two clauses: a base case and a recursive case (cf. Table 1.1). The choice of the solution strategy is an important design decision during creating a solution.

Note, other researchers may use different terms to describe the notion of *solution strategy* equivalently: for instance, *problem-solving procedure* (Mitrovic et al., 2007), programming technique (Hong, 2004), program schema (Gegg-Harrison, 1993), or programming plans (Johnson, 1990). In addition to solution strategies which lead to correct solutions, Ohlsson and Bee (1991) considered also inadequate solution strategies. Anticipating inadequate solution strategies is possible but difficult because they might be specific to a certain population of students (Vanneste, 1994). In this thesis, we only regard solution strategies which lead to correct solutions.

2.3.2 Implementation

Once a problem solver has decided to use a specific solution strategy to solve a given problem, she is faced with the issue of how to use the available means for the implementation. That includes finding out how the different available constructs of a particular domain can be applied and arranged in the context of the chosen solution strategy. If in the domain of travel planning, a problem solver has chosen the strategy of using a car, she can find many different routes by combining different roads. Or, if travelling by train, the planner also can combine different train connections to reach the desired destination. If a problem solver has decided for a solution strategy to solve the geometry problem above (e.g., using the theorem that the triangle ADE is isosceles if DE is parallel to BC), there are multiple ways to arrange the argument statements within a proof.

Similarly, in the domain of programming, a programmer has to apply the primitives of the programming language being used. On the implementation level the variability of a program is determined by the following factors:

1. The existence of semantically equivalent *syntactic reformulations* including the choice between alternative basic concepts: for instance, an arithmetic expression can be constructed

using different combinations of arithmetic operators (+, -, *, :, =, <, >, etc.); or explicit vs. implicit unification in Prolog; or before-incrementing (++i) vs. after-incrementing (i++) in Java).
2. The existence of *alternative sequential orderings* of programming constructs: within an implementation option, the sequential order of statements can sometimes be changed without changing the semantics. For instance, the order of subgoals and clauses in Prolog, or the order of statements in imperative programming languages).
3. The option to *introduce identifiers* according to individual preferences.
4. The possibility to *modularize a program* into simpler functional units by defining helper predicates (or functions).

As a result, to implement a solution strategy, there are numerous implementation variants (cf. Figure 1.1). In general, the solution space of a programming problem is open because it is not possible to anticipate all possible helper functions/predicates chosen by the student.

2.4 Classification of Problems

With respect to tutoring, given a limited set of solution strategies and formal constructs of a domain, a potentially very large space of solutions can be derived for a general problem. Based on the variability of solutions on the levels of solution strategy and implementation, Le et al. (2010) classified general problems into five classes according to an increasing size of the solution space. We adopt this classification for programming problems.

Class 1: one solution strategy, one implementation. Problems of this level can be solved only according to a single solution strategy and have only one solution. In many cases, the description for problems of this class can be specified in a way that the solution is unique. This kind of problems is suited to recall basic knowledge of the domain being taught because the unique solution can be used to address a concept which should be learned.

Class 2: one solution strategy, alternative implementation variants. On the second level, problems can be solved according to a single solution strategy which, however, can be implemented in many different ways. Problems on this level are typically precisely specified so that the space of possible solutions is narrowed down to a single solution strategy, or the input is restricted by pre-specified solution templates.

Class 3: a limited number of alternative solution strategies. In this class of problems, the student is free to choose one of several known alternative solution strategies and implements it according to her preferences. This kind of problems is more challenging than Class 2 and 3 because students have to make appropriate design decisions, i.e., choosing between solution strategies and implementation variants, instead of simply applying a predefined solution template. In the case that a student solution does not satisfy the requirements of a given problem, appropriate feedback can only be given to the student if the system has a reasonable hypothesis about the underlying solution strategy being most likely applied by the student.

Class 4: a great variability of possible solution strategies while the correctness of any given specific solution can still be verified. In this class, the problem is so complex that it needs to be solved by dividing it into sub-problems, which can be solved using different solution strategies. Since the combination of solution strategies results in a new solution strategy for the overall task, the number of these combinations is not known a priori.

Class 5: a great variety of possible solution strategies and the correctness of solutions cannot be verified. Problems of this class typically require solutions not only to fulfil certain testable functional requirements (cf. Class 4), but additionally their solutions should be considered "useful" and "acceptable" by a large number of stakeholders. The latter requirement usually results in controversial opinions which make solutions not formally verifiable.

2.5 Tutoring Systems for Programming

There exist numerous attempts to build tutoring systems for programming. However, few of them have been shown to be successful in helping students to improve their programming skills. Many systems have been reviewed in the studies of (Ducassé and Emde, 1988; Deek and McHugh, 1999). In this section, we take only systems into consideration, for which their effect of helping students or their diagnostic capability has been evaluated. We propose to classify them based upon the support phases for the process of programming and the possible variability of programming solutions. This classification aims at identifying the capability of existing tutoring systems for programming.

LISP-Tutor (Anderson and Reiser, 1985; Anderson et al., 1995): This tutor presents to the student a problem description containing highlighted identifiers for functions and parameters which have to be used in the implementation. To solve a programming problem, the student is provided with a structured editor which automatically balances parentheses and guides the student through a sequence of templates to be filled in. When the student types a LISP keyword, a new template is presented. If, for example, the construct *prog* (which can be used to implement an iteration) is entered, the tutor provides the following template:
(**prog** <LOCAL VARIABLES>
   <INITIALIZATIONS>
   <BODY>

2.5. TUTORING SYSTEMS FOR PROGRAMMING

< REPEAT>)

The symbols in angle brackets indicate place-holders that must be replaced by the student. Each student's input is monitored by the system. Whenever she makes a mistake, the tutor interrupts the process of programming and provides feedback immediately. The authors claimed that the system is able to support the student both during the implementation and the planning phase where the tutor works through the algorithm with the student step by step (Anderson and Reiser, 1985, p. 161), thus this system helps students acquire LISP primitives as well as basic programming concepts. The system allows the student to define new helper functions, but the intended purpose of the helper function has to be selected from a menu presented by the tutor. Moreover, an expression can be reformulated using different programming primitives. However, the student is neither allowed to apply alternative solution strategies to solve a given problem, nor to vary the sequential orderings of clauses in the prescribed templates. Only the argument positions within a slot of a template can be changed. This is considered a syntactic reformulation. It has been shown that students who used this system could achieve a certain competence level in 1/3 time compared to a traditional learning environment, and that the students who used this system for a period of one semester outperformed students in a corresponding control condition by an effect size of 1.0 standard deviation.

SQL-Tutor (Martin, 2001; Mitrovic et al., 2004): This tutor requests the student to define a SQL query to retrieve the appropriate data. SQL is not an universal programming language due to the underlying simple machine model. In fact, a SQL query is used to select data from a data base, but it cannot be used to process data like a program. For this reason, several database vendors devise their own languages, e.g., PL/SQL for Oracle, to enable software developers to query data, process them, and update the database accordingly.

When solving a problem, the system presents the student with a structured solution template which consists of pre-specified ordered slots for SQL constructs to be filled: SELECT, FROM, WHERE, GROUP BY, HAVING and ORDER BY (Mitrovic et al., 2004, p. 415). Thus, the system restricts the possibility of changing the order of SQL statements. However, it allows the student to apply alternative solution strategies as the authors stated: *"Constraint-based modelling can handle creativity because the student is free to use a novel problem-solving procedure without the system intervening"* (Mitrovic et al., 2007, p. 39), and there exists the possibility to reformulate the expression within an SQL statement. The system mainly supports students to construct a query for a given problem, this way, the student is able to acquire basic concepts of SQL[2]. This system has been shown being effective to help students improve their skills to define SQL queries: the students who used this tutor for two hours could improve their

---

[2] Comparable high level programming concepts in SQL cannot be identified.

skills by 0.65 standard deviation compared to the control group (Mitrovic and Ohlsson, 1999).

ELM-ART (Weber and Brusilovsky, 2001): This system for tutoring LISP is intended to help students on different skill levels. The users of ELM-ART have the choice among different support levels: listener, editor or exercise level. Among them, the listener level offers the least support: the student is allowed to solve a programming problem without any restriction (like solution templates). On the editor level, the student is presented with solution slots to fill in. On the exercise level, the student is similarly restricted like on the editor level, but has more support: the program of the student is evaluated dynamically using test cases. The system is intended to help students acquire the correct application of primitives and the basic concepts of LISP. The system provides three kinds of feedback: 1) information resulting from testing the solution using test cases, 2) results from error diagnosis in the code, and 3) similar examples to the given programming problem. The system is not able to support alternative solution strategies as the authors stated: *"for most of our exercises there is only one algorithm consisting of a single reference function"* (Weber and Möllenberg, 1995, p. 387). Therefore, the system supports only the possibility of syntactic reformulation to vary the implementation of a solution strategy. This system has been reported being effective in improving students' programming skills: the percentage of correct solutions to three final programming problems after completing six lessons in LISP using the system ELM-ART was between 87% and 96% (Weber and Brusilovsky, 2001, p. 377).

GIL (Reiser et al., 1988, 1992): The authors of this system promoted the idea of using a graphical representation for programs. That is, given a programming problem the student is requested to build a program by connecting objects representing program constructs together into a graph. The student is allowed to arrange the graphical objects in any way so that the resulting graph meets the problem's specification. The tutoring system monitors the student's problem solving and provides guidance upon request. This system is intended to help students in the planning phase to acquire basic concepts of LISP. It has been reported that students using GIL were able to reach similar levels of competence in about half the time in comparison to a corresponding control group (Reiser et al., 1992).

PROPL (Lane, 2004): The author introduced the notion of *pre-practice* tutoring which addresses the activities of analysing a task and planning a solution. The system does not support a specific programming language. Communication patterns were used to help students develop both an understanding of the problem and possible ways to solve it using pseudo language. Therefore, we were not able to identify whether it is possible to vary programming solutions on the implementation level. This system does not support alternative solution strategies, because for each problem the exercise author specifies *one* corresponding pseudo-code solution

2.5. TUTORING SYSTEMS FOR PROGRAMMING

(Lane and VanLehn, 2005, p. 7). PROPL has been evaluated with the programming languages Java and C (Lane and VanLehn, 2005, p. 10) and it has been reported that students who used this system were frequently better at creating algorithms for programming problems and demonstrated fewer errors in their implementation.

Table 2.2: A classification of tutoring systems for programming

System	ASS	SR	AO	MP	NI	Phase	Knowledge
LISP-Tutor		x		x	x	plan, impl.	primitives, basic
SQL-Tutor	x	x			-	impl.	primitives, basic
ELM-ART		x			x	impl.	primitives, basic
GIL		x			-	plan	basic
PROPL	-	-	-	-	-	analysis, plan	basic

ASS: alternative solution strategies; SR: syntactic reformulations; AO: alternative orderings; MP: modularizing programs; NI: naming identifiers.

Table 2.2 represents a classification of the tutoring systems for programming with respect to the solution variability. If a table cell is filled with the sign x or empty, indicating that a system supports a corresponding possibility of varying a solution or not, respectively. If a table cell is filled with the sign -, it means that no corresponding information was available. The table shows that most of the existing systems support the possibility of syntactic reformulations. None of the existing systems supports all aspects of solution variability (cf. Section 2.3). We also notice that only two systems (LISP-Tutor and PROPL) were intended to support different phases of the process of programming, and all of them focused rather on the primitives and basic programming concepts of a specific programming language than on high level programming knowledge.

Although all of the tutoring systems for programming mentioned above have been documented being effective in improving the programming skills of students, none of them has been evaluated with respect to their diagnostic capability. Indeed, these systems do not require a sophisticated diagnostic capability because they constrict the student's freedom due to the restricted ability of the underlying error diagnosis approach (Deek and McHugh, 1999), and thereby narrow down the possibilities to develop creative solutions. For instance, using the LISP-Tutor the student has to code a program in a top-down manner and the program is generated by the templates in a strictly left-to-right direction (Anderson and Skwarecki, 1986). GIL, a model-tracing system which supports students to construct graph-based programs, also restricts the student to a top-down problem solving manner. The SQL-Tutor offers the student more possibilities to vary a solution than the LISP-Tutor, the student is allowed to choose one of three alternative solution strategies[3]: a query can be defined by referencing a table either in the FROM clause, or in the WHERE clause, or in a JOIN expression (Martin, 2001, p. 35). The semantic correctness of a student solution is evaluated using an ideal solution which assumes that the student solution must contain certain structural components (which can be composed in different ways). In PROPL, the intention of the student is determined in the task analysis phase based on the selected communication patterns, thus error diagnosis was not necessary in this system.

There exist other systems, which attempted to support all possible sources of variability of solutions both on the solution strategy and the implementation level (Table 2.3). Although they have been evaluated with respect to their diagnostic capability, there is no evidence about their learning benefits. These systems can be referred to as *program analysers*. The column *Intention analysis* describes the capability of the systems to hypothesize the solution strategy underlying the student solutions correctly. This capability is also referred to as "program analysis" or "algorithm recognition" in the literature. The column *Diagnostic validity* describes the validity of error diagnosis of each system. The diagnostic validity usually depends on the results of intention analysis, because if the intention of the student is hypothesized wrongly, as a consequence, errors are detected based on that wrong hypothesis result.

From the table, it is obvious that the MENO-II system (Soloway et al., 1983) has poor diagnostic capabilities, because the system has been built with an anticipated library of errors for a simple programming task, but was evaluated using another more complex programming problem which resulted in a higher variability for implementing a solution. Except MENO-II, other systems like APROPOS2 (Looi, 1991), ADAPT Gegg-Harrison (1993), and Hong's tutor (Hong, 2004), which have been evaluated based on the single problem of reversing a list in Prolog, achieved a relatively high capability of hypothesizing the student's intention in over 80% of cases and a good rate of diagnostic validity (between 69% and 94%[4]). In particular, ADAPT has been tested on 125 student programs (including the 55 student programs given in (Looi, 1991)) and is able to recognize a larger set of correct solutions than APROPOS2. No information is available about how ADAPT has been evaluated, nor about its diagnostic capabilities.

PROUST(Johnson, 1990) has been evaluated based on two programming problems: the

---

[3]Mitrovic et al. (2004) used the notion of *problem-solving procedure*.
[4]This percentage is calculated by: $1 - \frac{No(NotDetected) + No(FalseAlarms)}{No(Errors)}$.

2.6. APPROACHES TO ERROR DIAGNOSIS

Rainfall[5] and the Bank problem[6]. The system has been reported being able to analyse[7] 81% of student programs for the first problem completely and to identify 94% of the bugs in these programs correctly. For the second problem, the accuracy of program analysis decreased to 50% while 91% of the bugs have been detected. According to the author, the result of intention analysis in the implementations for the Rainfall problem was better than the one for the Bank problem because the second problem required more complex solutions than the first one.

That these systems (cf. Table 2.3) have not been evaluated with respect to their learning benefits might be explained by the fact that they were built for a small number (between one and two) of programming problems. From the shortcomings of the systems described in Table 2.2 and Table 2.3 a need to focus on the following issues can be derived: 1) coaching the students in different phases of the programming process in addition to the implementation phase, 2) supporting the full range of variability of solutions for programming problems, and 3) communicating high level programming concepts to the students.

Table 2.3: Program analysers

System	Language	Intention Analysis	Diagnostic Validity
PROUST (Rainfall)	Pascal	81%	94%
PROUST (Bank)		50%	91%
MENO-II	Pascal	27%	-
APROPOS2	Prolog	80%	95%
ADAPT	Prolog	-	-
Hong's tutor	Prolog	80%	69%

2.6 Approaches to Error Diagnosis

In general, approaches to error diagnosis in programs can be classified into two groups. The first group includes the approaches which are specific to the domain of programming: plan and bug-based, and transformation-based techniques. We use the term *"program"* to describe the solution for a programming problem when discussing these specific approaches. The second

---

[5]The Rainfall problem requires writing a program in Pascal which prompts the user to input the amount of rainfall of a day, and calculate the average rainfall per day. Note: since rainfall cannot be negative, the program should reject negative input. The program should read data until the user types 99999. This is a sentinel value signalling the end of input.

[6]The Bank problem requires writing a Pascal program that processes three types of bank transactions: withdrawals, deposits, and a special transaction that says: no more transactions follow. The program should start by asking the user to input an account id and an initial balance.

[7]Johnson distinguishes between complete and partial analysis. An analysis is complete if a complete interpretation was generated, for which interpretation assessment could not find any inconsistencies. A partial analysis means that a part of the program was analysed. For comparing the capability between systems, we just compare the complete analyses of PROUST with other systems.

group includes general approaches, which can be applied in different domains: model-tracing and constraint-based techniques.

2.6.1 Library of Plans and Bugs

Although PROUST, ELM-ART, and APROPOS2 diagnose errors in programs implemented in different programming languages (Pascal, Lisp and Prolog), these systems work on the same principles: 1) modelling the domain knowledge using programming plans and buggy rules, 2) identifying the intention by matching the student program against anticipated programming plans, and 3) detecting errors using buggy rules which re-present common bugs made by students.

Each programming problem, which is posed to the student, is represented internally by a set of programming goals and data objects. Programming goals are the requirements which must be satisfied, while data objects are manipulated by the program. For example, the programming goal *Sentinel-Controlled-Input* (Johnson, 1990), which reads numbers in a sequence until some designated sentinel value is reached, can be specified like in Figure 2.3. The representation of programming goals has two important slots: *Form* and *Instances*. The slot *Form* shows the name of a possible function and two input parameters *?Input* and *?Stop* which represent the input and the sentinel values. The slot *Instances* indicates that this programming goal can be implemented using one of five different plans (Johnson, 1990).

```
(Goal-Definition Sentinel-controlled-Input
    InstanceOf        Read&Process
    Form              (Sentinel-Controlled-Input ?Input ?Stop)
    MainSegment       MainLoop:
    MainVariable      ?New
    NamePhrase        "sentinel-controlled loop"
    OuterControlPlan  T
    Instances         (Sentinel-Process-Read-While
                       Sentinel-Read-Process-While
                       Sentinel-Read-Process-Repeat
                       Sentinel-Process-Read-Repeat
                       Bogus-Counter-Controlled-Loop))
```

Figure 2.3: A definition for the goal Sentinel-Controlled-Input in PROUST.

A programming plan or an algorithm represents a way to implement a correspon-ding programming goal. To realize a goal, there might be more than one possible plan. In contrast to PROUST, APROPOS2 uses the concept of algorithms instead of programming plans. The author argues that the representation of programming plans is suited best for imperative languages like PASCAL where keywords for programming constructs, e.g., FOR-DO, or WHILE-DO, can

2.6. APPROACHES TO ERROR DIAGNOSIS

be used to anchor program analysis. Thus, he proposed to use algorithms as high level concepts in Prolog, and defined this notion as follows: *"An algorithm is a particular way of solving a problem that specifies a strategy for the problem's solution but leaves out details of the implementation"*. According to this definition, an algorithm is comparable to a composition of several programming plans. Figure 2.4 illustrates one sample plan which implements the goal *Sentinel-Controlled-Input*. This plan uses a WHILE loop to read in the value *?Input* until it agrees with the *?Stop* constant.

```
(Plan-Definition Sentinel-Process-Read-While
    Constants    (?Stop)
    Variables    (?Input)
    Template     ((SUBGOAL (Input ?Input))
                  (WHILE (< > ?Input ?Stop)
                    (BEGIN
                     ?*
                     (SUBGOAL (Input ?Input))))))
```

Figure 2.4: A plan for implementing the goal Sentinel-Controlled-Input in PROUST.

Common bugs are normally collected from empirical studies and represented as *buggy rules*. While PROUST contains only buggy rules, ELM-ART adds two more types: good and suboptimal rules which are used to comment good programs and less efficient programs (with respect to computing resources or time), respectively. APROPOS2 uses another representation of common bugs which are referred to as *buggy clauses*. Both buggy clauses and buggy rules serve the same purpose.

In general, a system of this class performs error diagnosis by synthesis in three steps. First, it looks up the problem description and identifies goals to be implemented. Second, it generates a variety of different ways to implement each goal, and derives hypotheses about the plans the programmer may have used to satisfy each goal. Each hypothesis is a possible correct program of the corresponding goal. Third, if the hypothesized plan matches the student program, the goal is implemented correctly. Otherwise, the system looks up the database of buggy rules to explain the plan discrepancies.

The procedure of error diagnosis in APROPOS2 exploits algorithms as high level programming concepts instead of programming plans and is carried out in a similar way. First, appropriate algorithms for a given problem are selected, and various possible programs are generated. Second, each generated program is matched against the student program, and the best algorithm is identified using a heuristic search technique. The third step employs buggy clauses to identify errors.

In principle, all three systems are able to identify the intention implemented in the student program using plan/algorithm matching, and detect errors using buggy rules/buggy clauses.

This approach has been proven useful to identify the intention underlying student program using programming plans. However, it is often criticized as being laborious, because a programming goal can be implemented according to many different programming plans and if a programming problem consists many programming goals to be satisfied, the space of combinations of programming plans would be very large. In addition, specifying buggy rules or buggy clauses requires an extensive study of misconceptions of the students. Such a study normally needs a large corpus of student programs. However, a library of buggy rules or buggy clauses might be specific to a certain population of students. Studies have shown that bug libraries cannot be used effectively with a new student population (Payne and Squibb, 1990). Johnson (1990) stated that PROUST was able to analyse the intention in 81% of the programs for the Rainfall problem which was assigned to a class of novice programmers (maybe at the Yale University, where the author was working). When this system was evaluated at two Belgian universities (UFSIA, Antwerpen and K.U. Leuven Campus Kortrijk), Vanneste (1994) reported that this rate dropped to less than 10%. To improve the ability to analyse programs created by a new student population, PROUST's library of buggy rules needs to be extended considering additional erroneous programming behaviours of the students.

2.6.2 Program Transformation

While the approach of using plan and bug libraries compares student programs to a set of anticipated correct programs and bugs, the transformation approach uses a single reference program to check the correctness of the student's one. The transformation approach can be divided into two classes: program-to-abstraction and program-to-program. In the first class, a student program and a reference program are transformed to higher level abstractions which are then compared to each other. In the second class, a reference program in normal form is transformed to the best representative one which is then compared to the student program.

Hong's Prolog tutor belongs to the first class. This system intends to transfer two kinds of programming knowledge to students: high level programming techniques[8] and basic programming concepts of logic programming. The domain model of the system consists of several high level programming techniques and each of them is represented by a set of grammar rules which are used to parse the student program. The system iteratively uses the sets of grammar rules to parse the student program. If the parsing procedure does not finish successfully, that means, the selected set of grammar rules has not been completely exploited and the strategy of the

---

[8]Actually Hong uses the term "programming technique" to describe high level concepts to solve a typical problem. This term might be confused with the notion of programming techniques proposed by Brna et al. (1999). To avoid this confusion, we use the term "high level programming techniques".

2.6. APPROACHES TO ERROR DIAGNOSIS

student program cannot be identified. In this case, the system uses one of the possible solution strategies specified for a given problem to guide the student. Otherwise, the solution strategy has been identified, and the system diagnoses errors in the student program. The system uses the same set of grammar rules, with which the solution strategy has been identified, to parse a corresponding reference program. For each possible solution strategy specified for a problem, there is a corresponding reference program. The parse tree of the student program is compared against the one for the reference program. The differences between the two parse trees indicate errors in the student program.

Whereas Hong's tutor transforms both the student and the reference program to higher-level abstractions, ADAPT transforms a Prolog program to another one (Gegg-Harrison, 1993). The error diagnosis process is divided into two steps. First, for a given problem, the system begins with a single reference program in normal form, generates a set of representative programs using a set of Prolog schemata (cf. Section 3.1.3). Then the algorithm underlying ADAPT transforms the most appropriate representative program into a structure that best matches the student program. The second step detects errors by matching the student program and the most representative one. If there are no mismatches, the student program is correct. Otherwise, the system attempts to explain mismatches by searching rules in the bug library. The program-to-program transformation model of ADAPT and the program-to-abstraction transformation model of Hong's tutor are illustrated by Figure 2.5.

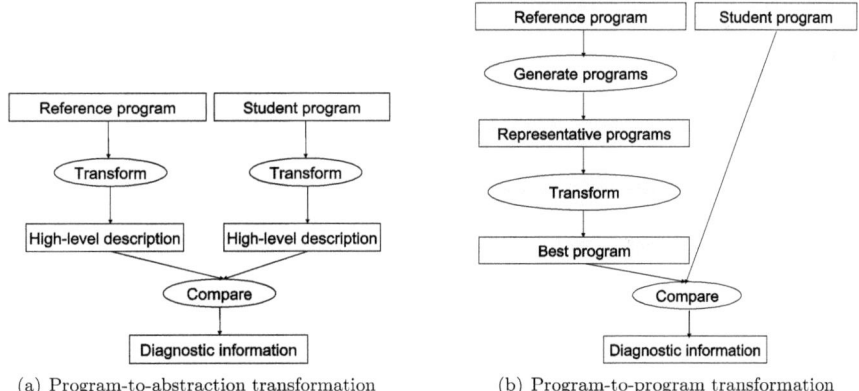

(a) Program-to-abstraction transformation   (b) Program-to-program transformation

Figure 2.5: Two different transformation models

The transformation approach is very comfortable for the author of an exercise because only one or a few reference programs are required, and specifying a reference program in normal form is a simple task. However, to the best of our knowledge, none of the systems mentioned above has been evaluated with respect to its effectiveness of tutoring. A possible explanation might be that a transformation algorithm is difficult to develop because it has to be verified that the transformed program produces the same results as the initial one. Even if there exists a transformation algorithm, it can only be used for a small class of programs. For example, ADAPT is only able to accept a class of programs for the list reversal problem[9].

2.6.3 Model-Tracing

The model-tracing approach is based on the cognitive theory ACT-R of skill acquisition (Anderson, 1993; Anderson et al., 1995). A *cognitive skill* can be conceived of as a subset of units of goal-related knowledge. The ACT-R theory can be summarized by means of three principal tenets:

1. There are two types of knowledge: *declarative* and *procedural*. In order to be able to solve a problem, some declarative knowledge is required. Declarative knowledge can be acquired by being told by a tutor or by reading a book, while procedural knowledge can only be acquired by performing a task.
2. Declarative knowledge can be converted into procedural one. The theory assumes that the student could exploit various types of instructions (e.g., feedback on errors, correction proposals, or analogy) to generate problem-solving behaviour. That is, the student is able to employ declarative knowledge to solve new problem tasks successfully.
3. Errors can be reduced. The theory claims that by practising with many problems of the same type, the student will produce fewer errors and construct a solution faster, because she has internalized this type of declarative knowledge and transformed it into procedural skills.

An elementary unit of procedural knowledge can be represented as a production rule which associates a problem solving situation (S) and a goal (G) with actions (A). The action A yields a new simpler situation and a smaller goal. For example, the following production rule recommends the sailor who is sailing in the evening (S): if he wants to sail to the west (G) he should follow the direction the sun is setting (A).

    IF   the goal is sailing to the west direction and it is evening,
    THEN sailing to the direction of the sunset

---

[9]The class of programs is defined by: "1) remove a single element from the front or back of their input list, 2) use simple variations of standard *append3* for input decomposition and output composition, 3) restrict the use of increasing arguments (i.e., arguments increase in length on each pass) to those that are necessary for the computation (e.g., accumulators) for outputs, 4) use a single recursive clause" (Gegg-Harrison, 1993, p. 8).

2.6. APPROACHES TO ERROR DIAGNOSIS

The core of a model-tracing tutoring system is the *cognitive model* which consists of problem-solving rules of an expert and typical erroneous behaviours of a population of students. Internally, a cognitive model is represented by a set of production rules which can be combined to form "ideal" and "buggy" solution paths for a certain problem (Anderson et al., 1995). An ideal solution path represents the problem solving rules which lead to a correct solution, while a buggy one anticipates possible erroneous students' problem solving steps. When the student inputs a solution, the system monitors her action symbol by symbol and generates a set of possible correct and buggy paths. Whenever a student's action can be recognized as belonging to a correct path, the student is allowed to go on. If the student's action deviates from the correct solution paths, the system generates instructions to guide the student towards a correct solution. Model-tracing tutors are able to give three types of feedback to students: flag feedback (also referred to as confirmation feedback in (Fleming and Levie, 1993), cf. Section 3.9), error explanation messages, and a chain of correction hints. The first type simply indicates the correctness of the student solution. An error explanation message is generated from an appropriate buggy rule which explains the error made by the student. If a student is stuck and needs help, she can request a hint to receive the first element of a chain of hints which suggests things the student should think about. If the student needs more help, she can continue to request a more specific hint until the last message is delivered that usually tells the student exactly what kind of action to perform. This type of feedback is generated from the information of the correct path which has been assumed to be the one the student is following (Heffernan et al., 2008). The model-tracing approach has been applied to building ITS not only in the domain of programming (e.g., the LISP-Tutor), but also in other domains such as Algebra (Corbett et al., 1997), and Physics (VanLehn et al., 2005).

With respect to diagnosing errors in student solutions, the model-tracing approach has demonstrated the following strengths in the LISP-Tutor. First, a model-tracing system is able to diagnose the student's intention by monitoring and relating the student's problem solving steps to the correct solution paths captured in the cognitive model (Anderson et al., 2010). Problem solving steps are derived based upon empirical research studies about how students learn to program LISP. A correct solution path in LISP programming is described as a sequence of problem solving steps which lead the problem solving process to a gradually simpler situation. For example, "If the goal is to combine LIST1 and LIST2 into a single list, THEN use the function APPEND and set as subgoals to code LIST1 and LIST2" (Anderson and Reiser, 1985) is a problem solving step which is necessary when the situation requires to concatenate two lists together. Whenever a problem solving step has not been carried out by the student successfully, the system can diagnose the error immediately even though only a partial solution is available so far. Second, correction hints which are generated from the "ideal" solution paths point to the next steps the student has to perform. Using this kind of information, the student can overcome impasses and go on with solving the given problem although she might not understand why she has to carry out that proposed step.

The model-tracing approach has been criticized as being too restrictive because of the following reasons (Anderson et al., 1995). First, the model-tracing approach tries to pull the student back on the paths leading to correct solutions, whenever the system diagnoses that the student's problem-solving step strays away from the correct solution paths or matches any buggy rule captured in the cognitive model. In principle, production rules can be used to model all possible correct solution paths, however, this would be a substantial task for modelling (Martin, 2001, p. 27). Thus, often only few solution paths are modelled, e.g., in the ACT programming tutor (Anderson et al., 1995). If the given problem is complex enough to be solved in many ways, e.g., a solution can be varied both on the solution strategy and implementation level, limiting the space of possible solutions to a few number of anticipated correct solution paths will exclude valid solutions (Deek and McHugh, 1999). Specifically, programming is a domain in which a student is allowed to create a program creatively. Researchers advocate the idea that programming learners should produce and debug errors in their programs in order to evolve their knowledge of programming and strengthen their problem solving skills (Eisenstadt et al., 1993; Vanneste, 1994). Limiting programming learners to certain solution paths restricts their creativity although it is arguable whether or not such a limitation affects learning.

Second, with respect to the process of programming, the model-tracing approach tends to support a linear problem solving process because the interaction style is very restrictive as researchers stated (Anderson and Skwarecki, 1986; Bonar and Cunningham, 1988). For example, using the LISP-Tutor, the student is requested to implement a program in a top-down and left-to-right manner. That is, after filling in a template correctly, a new template is presented to be completed. There is no possibility to go back to the last template for changes. In later model-tracing systems, e.g., Andes, a tutoring system for Physics (VanLehn et al., 2005), the student can also work with the mode *feedback-on-demand*, and is allowed to undo the last steps to correct her solution. In this case, a new solution path has to be established by the system. In case no solution path can be found, that is, the student may have performed an action that is neither on a correct path nor can it be interpreted by means of buggy rules, the approach may use repair theory to overcome this impasse (Brown and VanLehn, 1980), by backtracking and suggesting alternative actions. However, backtracking is non-trivial to implement since the point where to repair is rarely clear, and the repairer may encounter an exponential combinatorics of potential paths (Self et al., 1994). Using this mechanism,

2.6. APPROACHES TO ERROR DIAGNOSIS

the system would allow the student to derive her implementation in an iterative process of refinement and revision steps.

2.6.4 Constraint-based Modelling

While the model tracing approach focuses on the acquisition of cognitive skills based on procedural knowledge, the constraint-based approach is based on a "theory of learning from performance errors" (Ohlsson, 1996) which emphasizes the role of declarative knowledge. According to this theory, the learning process is divided into two phases.

In the first phase, it is expected that task-specific behaviour is generated. Like the ACT-R theory, two types of knowledge are distinguished: procedural[10] and decla-rative. The declarative knowledge is classified into *principled knowledge* and *factual knowledge*. The former consists of assertions about universals while the latter describes particular objects or events. The theory assumes that a student possesses some knowledge of both types prior to solving a problem. Adopting existing procedural knowledge, which might be general, the student performs a sequence of task-specific actions. She uses declarative knowledge to evaluate the performed actions. It is expected that the learner produces a lot of errors, because she is unfamiliar with a new problem type, although she possesses some knowledge for solving problems.

In the second phase, the theory assumes that a student is able to learn from her errors. An error is conceived of as a conflict between what the student believes to be true and what she perceives to be the case. For example, a sailor is trying to sail eastward (believe), but she encounters the sun sets in the sailing direction which indicates that she is moving in the wrong direction (perception). The student needs to go through two steps: 1) detecting errors, and 2) correcting errors. For error detection, principled knowledge is required. In the example of sailing a boat, the sailor catches the mistake by herself using the principled knowledge - that the sun rises from the east and sets in the west. Errors can also be pointed out by another person who might indicate that some principles of the task domain have been violated, and some executed actions should be corrected. Correcting errors also requires principled knowledge to identify the incorrectly performed actions and to recognize the situations which lead to initiating the actions. By revising the situations, such ineffective actions can be avoided in the future, and thus procedural knowledge becomes internalized.

The theory proposes that an elementary unit of principled knowledge is represented as a

---

[10] Actually, Ohlsson uses the term "practical knowledge" and avoids the term "procedural knowledge" because the latter is easily misunderstood as referring exclusively to knowledge about algorithms or formal procedures, even though the intended concept is the knowledge underlying action generally. For the purpose of comparison between the ACT-R and the theory of learning from performance errors, in this thesis the term "procedural knowledge" is used.

state constraint. Formally, a constraint C is an ordered pair <Relevance part, Satisfaction part> (Ohlsson and Rees, 1991). The *relevance part* describes the problem situation for which the constraint is relevant, and the *satisfaction part* encodes the conditions which have to be satisfied in order to fulfil the problem situation described in the relevance part. For example, the following constraint expresses a navigation principle of sailors:

IF   the evening is approaching and the sailor wants to sail in the west direction,

THEN   the sailor ought to follow the direction of the sunset.

Tutoring systems can be developed on the basis of constraints. The domain model of a constraint-based tutoring system is represented by a set of constraints. Constraints are used to model the principles of a specific domain and properties of correct solutions for a problem. Thus, constraints rather span a space of correct solutions (and a space of incorrect solutions) than model each correct solution. Given a student solution to be diagnosed, the relevant constraints are identified and evaluated. If the solution violates one or more constraints, the solution does not fall into the space of correct solutions, and the observed constraint violations are used as diagnostic information.

One of the advantages of the constraint-based approach is that it neither requires to enumerate every correct solution for modelling nor is it necessary to anticipate errors which can be made by the students (Ohlsson, 1994; Mitrovic et al., 2004). Instead, a limited number of domain principles and properties of correct solutions for a problem needs to be specified. Thus, from this point of view, using constraints to model the space of correct solutions for a programming problem, which can be solved by several thousands of implementation variants, is more appropriate than the model-tracing approach. Indeed, researchers have reported that the development of a model-tracing tutor requires more time and effort than a comparable constraint-based one for the same tutoring domain (Mitrovic et al., 2003; Kodaganallur et al., 2005).

With respect to the applicability of the constraint-based approach, Kodaganallur et al. (2005) stated that the constraint-based approach is applicable to problems which contain rich enough information in their solutions. For example, a solution for a statistical hypothesis testing problem is merely "reject" or "do not reject" a null hypothesis, and thus does not contain enough information for a constraint-based tutor to provide accurate feedback. On the contrary, a program contains rich information, and thus the constraint-based approach should be applicable to the domain of programming.

However, the constraint-based approach has several weaknesses which need to be addressed

2.6. APPROACHES TO ERROR DIAGNOSIS

when applying it to the domain of programming. First, constraints can be used to model all properties of correct solutions according to Ohlsson (1996), but they can become problem specific and relatively complex. For instance, the following constraint is specified to require that if the student intends to implement the analytic solution strategy (e.g., inv(S,R,P,Ret):-Ret is S*(R+1)^P.), then the exponent term of the analytic formula must be implemented correctly. Note that for the sake of simplicity, this constraint assumes that the order of the argument positions in the clause head is fixed.

IF   In the solution a calculation subgoal exists
AND one multiplication term exists on the RHS of the calculation
AND the multiplication term consists of two product factors
AND one product factor is a variable unified with the 1st argument position of the clause head
the second product factor is an exponential term

THEN   the exponent of the exponential term is unified with the 3rd argument position of the clause head
AND its basis is a sum of the value 1 and a variable unified with the 2nd argument position of the clause head

This constraint has been specified with five propositions in the relevance part and two in the satisfaction part. Such a highly specific constraint, whose relevance part contains many conditions, tends to fail in erroneous situations, because its relevance part is not robust against minor deviations from the specified situation. A complex constraint with a conjunction of conditions in the relevance part becomes irrelevant for a student solution, if only a single one of the conjuncts fails. Thus, the constraint can be satisfied even though this undesired result might have been caused by another error elsewhere in the student solution. This leads to the paradox that constraints that are meant to diagnose errors can be completely neutralized by other errors. The potential that complex constraints might become useless is obvious when specifying constraints for the domain of programming.

Instead of specifying problem-specific requirements in constraints, Ohlsson and Mitrovic (2006) suggested to use an *ideal solution* which is meant to capture the characteristics of correct solutions and constraints have to be specified to compare the necessary components of the ideal solution with the components of a student solution. This way is similar to other approaches to error diagnosis. The plan-based approach, for instance, uses a set of programming plans to anticipate possible algorithms for a given problem. The transformation approach needs a reference program to compare it with the student solution. In model-tracing tutors, this is achieved by specifying an expert model which consists of possible solution paths.

The approach of using an ideal solution to encapsulate the semantic requirements of solutions to a problem has the advantage that complex constraints can be avoided to a certain extent. Furthermore, it is not necessary to specify new constraints for a new exercise because problem-specific requirements are contained in the ideal solution of that exercise, assuming that the existing set of constraints can cover the learning domain sufficiently.

However, choosing an ideal solution among many alternatives for a programming problem is not an easy task. In addition, even if an ideal solution could be identified, the strategy underlying the ideal solution might not agree with the student's intention, and the resulting diagnostic information would mislead students. This problem has been identified by (Martin, 2001, p.43) when investigating the applicability of the CBM approach in the domain of SQL, as well discussed in (Kodaganallur et al., 2006, p. 321) and (Woolf, 2009, p. 85). This is the second shortcoming of the constraint-based approach. To solve this problem, Martin (2001) suggested a reverse engineering technique which uses elements of an ideal solution and information from each violated constraint in order to construct a correct solution on the basis of the student solution. This technique aims at developing a problem solver to generate a correct solution which follows the same solution strategy as the one of the student solution, and correction hints are based on the generated correct solution. This technique works well in the domain of SQL, however, it remains an open question whether this technique can be applied to other domains (Martin, 2001, p. 8). Developing a problem solver could be possible for rather simple problem domains (Mitrovic et al., 2007, p. 40), however, in many domains it can be very difficult. Indeed, building a problem solver for programming problems is an issue which still does not have a solution. So far, various code generators have been developed, however, they can only generate a frame of code. Human programmers are required to adjust the generated code to satisfy the requirements of a problem. Furthermore, in a complex domain like programming, the implementation of two different solution strategies for a given programming problem can be totally different, i.e., some components required by a solution strategy may not be needed in the implementation of another solution strategy (e.g., the implementation of the tail recursive strategy vs. the analytic solution strategy in Table 1.1). Therefore, the approach of applying the reverse engineering technique to build a problem solver for the domain of programming cannot be promising.

This problem raises the need to hypothesize the strategy underlying a solution during the process of diagnosing errors. Thus, it is required to enhance a constraint-based tutoring system for programming with the capability of diagnosing errors in accordance with the student's intention. The issue of identifying the student's intention also occurs in model-tracing systems: the student's problem solving steps are matched against paths of cognitive actions captured in

2.6. APPROACHES TO ERROR DIAGNOSIS

the cognitive model. Whenever, for instance, the LISP-Tutor has difficulties to select a path of the student's problem solving from a set of alternatives, the student is requested to identify the proper interpretation of her action from a disambiguation menu.

Neither the constraint-based nor the model-tracing approach provide appropriate means to distinguish severe errors from minor ones. Model-tracing systems tend to present a feedback message immediately whenever the student' problem solving step deviates from the expert model whereas constraint-based systems tend to present a list of errors in arbitrary order. Here, a selection criterion is needed.

The constraint-based approach has another weakness with respect to the quality of feedback. Researchers agree that a model-tracing tutoring system can provide a more comprehensive and goal-targeted feedback than a comparable CBM system (Mitrovic et al., 2003; Kodaganallur et al., 2005). This claim is true due to two reasons. First, in addition to error explanation messages which are generated from buggy rules, the expert model of a model-tracing system is able to provide the student with a sequence of problem solving actions, which force her to always stay on a correct solution path, while a constraint-based system only provides explanations of a possible error. Nevertheless, a constraint-based tutoring system can also provide corrective feedback messages through processing diagnostic information. Menzel (1992), for instance, combined diagnostic results to generate corrective hints in the domain of natural language grammar. Note, that a model-tracing system can provide corrective feedback in addition to error explanations, but has to pay a higher cost (Mitrovic et al., 2003; Kodaganallur et al., 2005). That is because the development of an expert model of the model-tracing system requires to enumerate each possible solution path, and the library of buggy rules needs to anticipate all possible errors the students may produce. If a model-tracing system allows the student to develop a program in a creative way, that is, a solution can be varied on the level of the solution strategy and the implementation level, creating a cognitive model for the domain of programming would not be an easy task.

The second reason for the lower quality of constraint-based feedback is that constraints model knowledge units (e.g., domain principles) which are largely unrelated to each other, and thus the feedback messages generated from constraint violations may become incoherent. For example, two basic principles in the domain of logic programming are: 1) If a calculation subgoal is implemented, then the operator **is/2** is used; 2) If a recursive case is implemented, then there exists an input variable which is decomposed recursively in the clause body. If a minor error exists in a solution, e.g., the third subgoal of the second clause of the tail recursive implementation (`NP is P-1`, cf. Table 1.1) is wrongly coded like `NP = P-1`, then constraints which model these two principles (and many others) will be violated. The first constraint is violated because in logic programming, this code is interpreted as a unification (due to the operator =) while a calculation subgoal is expected. The second constraint is violated, because a subgoal which decomposes a value (if the input variable is a list) or decrements it (if the input variable is a number) is required to implement a recursive case, but the wrongly coded subgoal does not satisfy this requirement.

2.6.5 A Summary of The State of The Art

We have investigated four of the most promising approaches to error diagnosis in tutoring systems for the domain of programming: using a library of plans and bugs, program transformation, model-tracing, and constraint-based modelling. Table 2.4 summarizes the first two approaches and their (dis)advantages.

Table 2.4: Plans and bugs-based vs. program transformation-based approach

	Plans and bugs	**Program transformation**
Modelling techniques	programming plans, algorithms, buggy rules, clauses	reference programs transformation algorithm (TA)
Intention analysis	plan/algorithm matching	capable
Error detection	buggy rules/clauses	program/abstraction matching
Ranking of errors	not capable	not capable
(Dis)advantages	laborious modelling (a library of plans & bugs)	comfortable modelling (few reference programs) a TA is applicable to a small class of programs

While the approach of using a library of plans and bugs and the transformation-based approach simply serve the purpose of error diagnosis specific for the domain of programming, the model-tracing and the constraint-based approaches are based on cognitive learning theories and can be applied to different domains. Table 2.5 summarizes these approaches and their (dis)advantages with respect to developing tutoring systems for the domain of programming.

The next chapter will propose solutions to enhance the diagnostic capability of the constraint-based approach to be able to analyse student's intention during the process of error diagnosis and to rank the severity of diagnosed errors.

2.6. APPROACHES TO ERROR DIAGNOSIS

Table 2.5: Model-tracing vs. constraint-based approach

	Model-tracing	Constraint-based
Cognitive theory	ACT-R	learning from errors
Modelling techniques	production/buggy rules	constraints
Modelling work	more laborious	less laborious
Intention analysis	path tracing	not sufficient
Error detection	buggy rules	constraint violations
Ranking of errors	not capable	not capable
Feedback	more goal-directed (explanatory & corrective)	less goal directed (tend to be explanatory) (can be corrective)

Chapter 3

A Coaching System For Logic Programming

Since students experience different difficulties when solving programming problems, it would be helpful to provide them guidance according to the programming phases. Therefore, the first purpose of this chapter is to present *a two-stage coaching strategy* as a tutoring model: task analysis prior to implementation.

The second purpose of this chapter is to propose an approach to *model the solution space for a programming problem in a tutoring system for logic programming and diagnose errors in logic programs accurately through the use of weighted constraints*. To model the solution space, two additional model components are required: a semantic table and a set of transformation rules. The semantic table represents the semantic information required to solve a problem. Constraints are used to check the semantic correctness of the student solution with respect to the requirements specified in the semantic table and examine general well-formedness conditions. Transformation rules extend the space of solutions further. In addition, the approach presented here adopts soft computing techniques for solving constraint satisfaction problems in order to enhance the capabilities of error diagnosis. For that purpose, each constraint is associated with a constraint weight, a heuristic information indicating the importance of the constraint. Primarily, constraint weights serve to control the process of error diagnosis. In addition, they are used to hypothesize the strategy implemented in the student solution and to rank feedback messages according to the severity of diagnosed errors.

All design proposals made in this chapter have been implemented in a system (INCOM), which is used to test the hypotheses specified in Chapter 1.

3.1 Logic Programming - A Case Study

Logic programming is based on first order logic. A logic program is composed of *facts* and *rules*. Facts describe the relationships between objects, and a rule defines a new relationship based on existing relationships (Sterling and Shapiro, 1994, p. 11, 18). Although, logic programming languages are declarative ones, a logic program can be viewed both declaratively and procedurally. From the declarative view, a fact is represented by a n-tuple relationship and a rule can be conceived of as a conjunction of existing relationships. From the procedural view, a rule can be regarded as a sequence of function calls, and a logic program can be interpreted as a procedure of instruction statements.

3.1.1 Simplified Prolog

Following the goal of helping students to acquire basic and high level concepts in logic programming, we restrict our attention to a subset of the language Prolog in order to avoid a too high cognitive load of programming beginners and to provide them with plausible feedback about errors occurred in their solutions. This subset includes built-in predicates and functions as well as the operators: =, =:=, =\=, ==, \==, >, >=, <, =<, =.., +, -, *, /, ^. Moreover, '**is**' can be used to evaluate arithmetic expressions. Although this set of built-in predicates and functions is relatively small, it can be used to solve a large range of programming problems. According to text books for Prolog (e.g., Brna (2001)), higher-order predicates including declarative predicates (e.g., findall/3, bagof/3, setof/3) and non-declarative ones (e.g., assert/1, retract/1 used to manipulate the database) are normally tutored once students have learned the primitive built-in predicates.

A Prolog program contains several predicate definitions, each of them is composed of one or more *clauses*. A clause representing a fact consists of only a *clause head*, whereas a clause representing a rule consists of a clause head and a *clause body*. The clause body is composed of several *subgoals* which represent a conjunction of relationships. Each subgoal in turn has a *functor* and several *arguments*. If an argument represents an arithmetic expression, it is regarded as a summation of terms which can be decomposed according to the following rules. Note, we consider only a limited subset of arithmetic expressions:

3.1. LOGIC PROGRAMMING - A CASE STUDY

summation	:=	multiplication-term | multiplication-term algebraic-sign summation
multiplication-term	:=	[algebraic-sign] product-factor | [algebraic-sign] product-factor {*, /} multiplication-term
product-factor	:=	base-item | exponential-term
exponential-term	:=	base-item ^ base-item
base-item	:=	variable | number
algebraic-sign	:=	+ | -

Figure 3.1 illustrates the structural hierarchy of a predicate. The hierarchy has five levels: clauses on the first, clause head and subgoals on the second, functor and arguments on the third, multiplication terms on the fourth, algebraic sign and product factors on the fifth level.

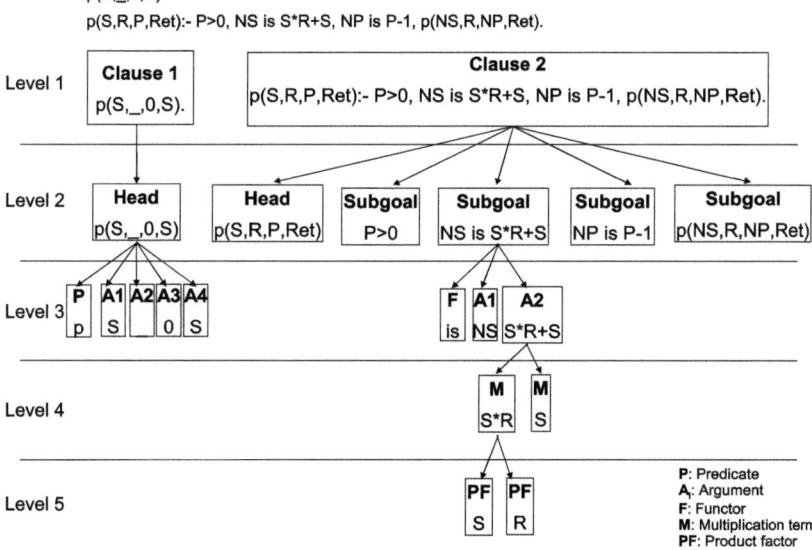

Figure 3.1: The structural hierarchy of a Prolog predicate.

3.1.2 Solution Space

Despite the small set of built-in predicates mentioned above, Prolog allows us to create a large solution space for a logic programming problem. In the following, we discuss the factors which determine a solution space (cf. Section 2.3) to the case of logic programming.

Syntactic reformulation

Each subgoal is associated with a role: *(de)composition, recursion, calculation, arithmetic test, unification, term test,* or *user-defined*. A role of a subgoal can be implemented in different ways. We define the role of each subgoal type formally based on the terminology and notation in (Lloyd, 1987).

C_i is a clause.

Θ is a list of subgoals.

S_i is a subgoal.

t_i, u_i are terms.

x, y, z are variables.

c_i is an atom.

A *(de)composition subgoal* composes an argument using other variables or decomposes an argument into several variables or constants. A (de)composition can be established implicitly at an argument position or can be represented explicitly as a separate subgoal. List is the most frequently used data structure for (de)composition.

Definition 3.1.1 *Let X be a clause of the form $p(t_1,...,t_n)$:-Θ. t_i ($1 \leq i \leq n$) is an* implicit *(de)composition if $t_i = [x_1,..,x_q|y]$ ($1 \leq q$) or $t_i = [x_1,..,x_m]$ ($1 < m$).*

Definition 3.1.2 *Let X be a clause of the form $p(t_1,...,t_n)$:-Θ. t_i ($1 \leq i \leq n$) is an* explicit *(de)composition if t_i is a variable z, $z = [x_1,..,x_q|y] \in \Theta$ ($1 \leq q$) or $z = [x_1,..,x_m] \in \Theta$ ($1 < m$).*

Definition 3.1.3 *Let X be a clause of the form $p(t_1,...,t_n)$:-Θ. If t_i ($1 \leq i \leq n$) is an* explicit *(de)composition, t_i is a variable z, $z = [x_1,..,x_q|y] \in \Theta$ ($1 \leq q$) or $z = [x_1,..,x_m] \in \Theta$ ($1 < m$), then a variant of (de)composition is an* implicit *(de)composition on the argument position t_i for which the following condition holds: $t_i = [x_1,..,x_q|y]$ or $t_i = [x_1,..,x_m]$.*

Let X be a clause of the form $p(t_1,...,t_n)$:-Θ. If t_i ($1 \leq i \leq n$) is an implicit *(de)-composition, $t_i = [x_1,..,x_q|y]$ ($1 \leq q$) or $t_i = [x_1,..,x_m]$ ($1 < m$), then a variant of (de)composition is an* explicit *(de)composition on the argument position t_i for which the following conditions hold: 1) t_i is a variable z; 2) $z = [x_1,..,x_q|y]$ or $z = [x_1,..,x_m]$ is a subgoal in the clause body.*

For example, the argument position X in the clause `p(X,Y):-X=[H|T], p(T,Y).` is (de)composed into a list `[H|T]` explicitly according to Definition 3.1.2, and the first argument position of this clause `p([H|T],Y):-p(T,Y).` is (de)composed implicitly according to Definition 3.1.1.

A *recursive subgoal* has the same functor and the same arity as its clause head. The following definition for recursive subgoals includes both decreasing recursion and increasing recursion defined by Gegg-Harrison (1993).

3.1. LOGIC PROGRAMMING - A CASE STUDY

Definition 3.1.4 *Let X be a clause of the form $p(t_1,...,t_n)$:-Θ. If $\exists p(u_1,..,u_n) \in \Theta$, then $p(u_1,..,u_n)$ is a recursive subgoal in X*

A *calculation subgoal* is used to evaluate an arithmetic expression using the operator "**is**".

Definition 3.1.5 *t_a is an arithmetic expression if ϑ is the set of operators which are used in this expression and $\forall \varepsilon \in \vartheta, \varepsilon \in \{+,-,*,/,\hat{}\}$*

Definition 3.1.6 *S is a calculation subgoal if $\exists S \in \Theta$ and S has the form t_x **is** t_a where t_a is an arithmetic expression and t_x is either a numeric atom or a variable.*

The calculation subgoal t_x **is** t_v is a variant of S if t_a can be transformed to t_v applying the distributive and commutative laws of mathematics. For example, applying the distributive and commutative law to the arithmetic expression `S is M*X+N*X`, it can be transformed to: `S is (M+N)*X`, or `S is X*N+M*X`.

An *arithmetic test subgoal* is used to compare two instantiated arguments which are of type number. There are two classes of arithmetic test subgoals. The first one applies the operators: $<, >, =<$ and $>=$ to test whether a number is greater/smaller than another one. The second class applies the operators: $=:=$ and $=\backslash=$ to test whether two expressions evaluate to the same number or not.

Definition 3.1.7 *rev_o is a function which finds a reverse operator for an arithmetic comparator according to the following rules:*

- $rev_o(>) = <$
- $rev_o(<) = >$
- $rev_o(=<) = >=$
- $rev_o(>=) = =<$

Definition 3.1.8 *If S is an arithmetic test subgoal $t_x \doteq t_y \in \Theta$, $\doteq \in \{=:=, =\backslash=\}$, and t_x, t_y are arithmetic expressions, then $t_y \doteq t_x$ is a variant of S.*

If S is an arithmetic test subgoal $t_x \triangleleft t_y \in \Theta$, $\triangleleft \in \{=<, >=, >, <\}$, and t_x, t_y are arithmetic expressions, the following expressions are variants of S where $rev_o(\triangleleft) = \triangleright$:

- $t_y \triangleright t_x$
- $t_x - t_y \triangleleft 0$
- $t_y - t_x \triangleright 0$
- $0 \triangleright t_x - t_y$,
- $0 \triangleleft t_y - t_x$

According to Definition 3.1.8, an arithmetic test subgoal whose operator is an element of the set $\{=:=, =\backslash=\}$ can be reformulated by transposing its arguments. An arithmetic test subgoal, whose operator is an element of the set $\{=<,>=,>,<\}$, for example, `X<Y`, can be reformulated in one of the following forms: `Y>X, X-Y<0, Y-X>0, 0>X-Y, 0<Y-X`.

A *unification subgoal* unifies two structures, or two variables, or assigns a value to a variable using the operator $=$. The unification subgoal is referred to as an explicit unification. A unification can also occur if two different argument positions have the same variable name or variables within two terms at the argument positions have the same name. This case is called implicit unification or co-reference. For instance, there is an implicit unification in the clause `member(H, [H|T])`. using the co-reference variable H at two argument positions, whereas the clause `member(X,[H|T]):-X=H`. uses a subgoal to unify two argument positions explicitly. We define the two variants of unification formally:

Definition 3.1.9 *Let X be a clause of the form $p(t_1,...,t_n)$:-Θ. v_i is a set of variables existing in term t_i and v_j is a set of variables existing in term t_j, ($1 \leq i,j \leq n, i \neq j$). There exists an implicit unification between two arguments in t_i and t_j if $\exists x, x \in v_i$ and $x \in v_j$.*

Definition 3.1.10 *Let X be a clause of the form $p(t_1,...,t_n)$:-Θ. v_i is a set of variables existing in term t_i and v_j is a set of variables existing in term t_j, ($1 \leq i,j \leq n, i \neq j$). There exists an explicit unification between two arguments in t_i and t_j if*

- $\exists x \in v_i \wedge \exists y \in v_j, x \neq y$,

- $\exists x \diamond y \in \Theta$ or $\exists y \diamond x \in \Theta$ where $\diamond$ is the unification operator $=$

A *term test subgoal* is used to test whether two terms are equivalent using the operators: `==` and `\==`. We also include the operator `\=` into the class of term test because it tests whether two terms are not unifiable. The arguments of a term test subgoal can be transposed without changing the semantics of the subgoal.

Definition 3.1.11 *S is a term test subgoal $x \circ y \in \Theta$, if $\circ \in \{==, \backslash==, \backslash=\}$. $y \circ x$ is a variant of S.*

A subgoal is considered *user-defined* if the student defines a helper predicate explicitly which is called by its main predicate. We will discuss the role of helper predicates in Section 3.1.2.

Definition 3.1.12 *Let X be a clause of the form $p(t_1,...,t_n)$:-Θ_1, Y be a clause of the form $p(t_{v1},...,t_{vn})$:-Θ_2. Y is a syntactic reformulation of X,*

- *if $\exists t_i$, ($1 \leq i \leq n$), t_i is a (de)composition and $\exists t_{vi}$ is a variant of (de)composition of t_i;*
- *if there is an unification between two arguments in t_i, t_j ($1 \leq i,j \leq n$, $i \neq j$), and there is a variant of unification between two arguments in t_{vi}, t_{vj};*
- *if S is an arithmetic test subgoal $\exists S \in \Theta_1$ and $\exists S_v \in \Theta_2$, S_v is a variant of S;*
- *if S is a calculation subgoal $\exists S \in \Theta_1$ and $\exists S_v \in \Theta_2$, S_v is a variant of S;*

3.1. LOGIC PROGRAMMING - A CASE STUDY

- if S is a term test subgoal $\exists S \in \Theta_1$ and $\exists S_v \in \Theta_2$, S_v is a variant of S.

Alternative Sequential Ordering

Since a rule can be interpreted as a sequence of logical relationships, from the declarative perspective, the ordering of subgoals within a clause and clauses within a predicate can be rearranged without changing the semantics of a logic program. Nevertheless, efficiency might be an issue, because the order of clauses affects the search space of the Prolog interpreter. The issue of termination is also important. Since the interpreter of a logic programming language processes a logic program procedurally, not always the permutation of a program leads to a new program which can safely terminate. The problem of detecting infinite loops in general logic programs is not decidable, although several attempts have been made to prove the termination properties for a restricted class of logic programs (Bol, 1995; Gelder, 1989). Since logic programming languages are declarative, we allow students to arrange the order of subgoals and clauses freely, except in cases where an arithmetic subgoal (arithmetic test or calculation) is used. In such a case, the order of subgoals within a clause must be kept because the variables in this subgoal must have been instantiated before they can be processed. We define alternative sequential ordering variants for subgoals within a clause and clauses within a program formally as follows:

Definition 3.1.13 *An ordering $>_o$ on a set of subgoals (or clauses) is a sequence $S_1 >_o S_2 >_o S_3 >_o ...$ of subgoals (clauses).*

Definition 3.1.14 *$\exists S_i, S_j \in \Theta, (i \neq j)$, $S_i, S_j \notin \{\text{calculation, arithmetic test}\}$, alternative sequential ordering variants of S_i and S_j are $S_i >_o S_j$ and $S_j >_o S_i$.*

Definition 3.1.15 *If $C_i, C_j (i \neq j)$ are two clauses of a program, alternative sequential ordering variants of C_i and C_j are $C_i >_o C_j$ and $C_j >_o C_i$.*

Definition 3.1.16 *I is an implementation of a predicate. J is a variant of I*

- *if a clause of J is a syntactic reformulation of a clause of I;*

- *if the sequential ordering of subgoals within a clause of J is an alternative sequential ordering of subgoals within a clause of I;*

- *if the sequential ordering of clauses within the implementation of J is an alternative sequential ordering of clauses of I.*

Solution Strategy

In 2.3.1 we have intuitively defined the term *solution strategy*. Here, we characterize this notion more formally. Note, the formal definition of this term is specific and serves to design our coaching system for logic programming. It is not used to compare the complexity of programming problems provided by different tutoring systems.

Definition 3.1.17 α *is a* solution strategy *to a problem. If I is an implementation of* α*, then the variants of I are also implementations of* α*.*

Definition 3.1.18 *Two solution strategies* α *and* β *to solve a problem can be called* different *if* χ *and* ψ *are the sets of implementation variants of* α *and* β*, then* $I \in \chi \rightarrow I \notin \psi$*.*

Helper Predicates

A Prolog programmer has the possibility to modularize a program by defining new helper predicates which are called as subgoals in the clause body of the main predicate. Formal definitions for helper predicates and main predicates can be found in (Gegg-Harrison, 1993). There are two cases where a helper predicate is necessary: 1) modularising a program in functional units which can be reused, and 2) defining an accumulative predicate. The first case is illustrated by the following example. The task of determining a list of persons (each element of the person list is a pair of name and age) whose age is greater than 18 can be implemented in *adult/2* using the helper predicate *greater18/1*:

```
adult([],[]).
adult([(N,A)|T], [(N,A)|R]):-greater18(A), adult(T,R).
adult([(N,A)|T], R):-adult(T,R).
greater18(X):-X >= 18.
```

An accumulative predicate is a special form of a helper predicate which accumulates a series of values recursively into an argument. For example, the predicate *sum/2* which sums all integer elements of a list can be implemented by defining an accumulative predicate *sumAcc/3* which accumulates all integer elements into an accumulator argument and passes the accumulator value to the result argument when the list is empty.

```
sum(List, Result):-sumAcc(List, Result, 0).
sumAcc([], Sum, Sum).
sumAcc([H|T], Sum, Accu):- NewAccu is Accu+H, sumAcc(T, Sum, NewAccu).
```

Introducing Identifiers

The last possibility of varying a program is the option of introducing identifiers. Like in all programming languages, a Prolog programmer is able to name a predicate or variables according to her individual understanding.

3.1. LOGIC PROGRAMMING - A CASE STUDY

3.1.3 High Level Programming Knowledge

Prolog Schemata

A *Prolog schema* is a generalization of a class of Prolog programs which share a common structure. The syntactic structure of a Prolog program represents a parti-cular function. Gegg-Harrison (1999) has developed fourteen solution schemata which can be used to solve a range of typical list processing problems in Prolog. For example, the following *schema A* describes a class of programs whose goal is to access and process every element of a list. *length/2*, *sum/2*, and *reverse/2*, which should count the length of a list, sum all integer elements of a list, and reverse a list, respectively, share the same schema A.

schema_A([], <<&1>>).
schema_A([X|Xs], <<&2>>):-
<pre_pred(<<&3>>,X,<<&4>>),>
schema_A(Xs, <<&5>>)
<,post_pred(<<&6>>,X,<<&7>>)>.

To describe schemata, Gegg-Harrison devised a schema language. In addition to normal Prolog constructs and variable representation, the schema language employs schema variables << &1 >>,...,<< &7 >> which represent place holders for any number of data arguments. The *pre_pred* and *post_pred* components exemplify subgoals which are invocated before or after calling the recursive subgoal. The single brackets indicate that the existence of *pre_pred* and *post_pred* are optional.

Prolog programming techniques

Opposed to Prolog schemata, which represent standard structures of Prolog programs, *Prolog programming techniques* capture semantic relationships and are normally used by Prolog experts in a systematic way to achieve a certain computation. As such, programming techniques say something about the computation being undertaken rather than simply providing a syntactic pattern. Programming techniques can be used in different contexts. For instance, decomposing a list is a Prolog programming technique which can be applied to count the elements of a list or to double the integer elements of a list. A technique can be so basic that it applies to only parts of a complete procedure, e.g., the *same* technique requires two arguments to be co-referenced, i.e., to share the same value; or the *list-head* technique describes an argument whose value in the head is the list and whose value in the recursive subgoal is its tail (Bowles and Brna, 1999). Several basic techniques can be combined together in a procedure and build a new more complex technique, e.g., the *test-for-existence* technique, which is used to determine that a list of objects has at least one object with a specified property, is composed of many basic techniques (Brna et al., 1999).

Prolog Patterns

Since a Prolog schema represents common solutions for a class of typical problems, it can be considered a Prolog pattern. In general, a pattern describes a space of similar problems and a space of solutions, which have worked well in the past and can be applied again to similar problems in the future (Beck et al., 1996). The term *pattern* has been adopted in the software development from the work of Christopher Alexander, who was exploring patterns in architecture (Alexander, 1979). Gamma et al. (1995) devised design patterns for the paradigm of object-oriented programming.

Similarly, there exist patterns in designing Prolog programs. Brna (2001) defined four Prolog patterns which can be applied to solve problems using recursion:

- *Test-all-elements*: If the problem is to determine whether all elements of a collection (e.g., a list) have a desired property, then this pattern can be applied.
- *Test-for-existence*: Similarly to the previous pattern, this one is used to check whether at least one object of a collection (e.g., a list) has a desired property.
- *Process-all-elements*: This pattern describes the standard solution for the problem of processing all elements of a collection.
- *Process-all-accumulator*: This pattern exploits the tail recursive strategy (cf. Section 1.3) to solve the same class of problems as the pattern *Process-all-elements*.

For example, if the problem consists in processing all elements of a list, we can use the pattern *Process-All-Elements* to define a predicate. The structure of this pattern corresponds to schema A mentioned previously. The semantics of this pattern can be described as follows:

- in case the input list is empty, the result of processing the elements in this list is an empty list (for list processing) or 0 (for arithmetic processing);
- in other cases (the input list is not empty), the rest of the list is processed, and the total result of the whole list is constructed (or calculated) by processing the head of the list and the result of the rest list.

Since a Prolog pattern can be specialised by inheriting the characteristics of a super-pattern and adding new Prolog programming techniques, patterns can be organised in a hierarchy (Figure 3.2) as proposed in (Hong, 2004)[1].

---

[1] Actually, Hong (2004) organised programming techniques in a hierarchy.

3.2. REQUIREMENTS

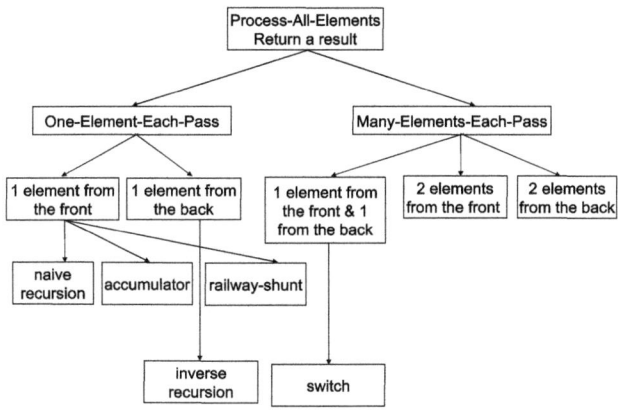

Figure 3.2: A small hierarchy of Prolog patterns.

3.2 Requirements

To investigate the applicability of the constraint-based modelling approach for building tutoring systems in the domain of programming, we develop a tutoring system for logic programming. This system is intended to help students of a logic programming course solve homework exercises. The system is required to have the following characteristics, while the arguments for these requirements are discussed in the subsequent sections:

1. **Tutoring strategy:** Since students may have difficulties during different phases of the programming process, coaching is required in each of these phases (with the focus on the analysis and implementation phases) to help students solve programming problems.

2. **Problem Types:** In this thesis we focus on programming problems which require the skills to define predicates using facts and rules. In particular, the application of recursive programming techniques is emphasized, because for most novice programmers recursion is a difficult programming concept (Haynes, 1995). Students are provided with programming problems which may be solved by applying several different solution strategies (which can be anticipated) and each solution strategy can be implemented in many variants. Students are allowed to develop creative solutions for this type of problems, that is, they have the possibility to apply alternative solution strategies, choose syntactic reformulations, vary alternative sequential orderings of subgoal/clause, define new helper predicates, and to

introduce identifiers of their choice for variables or predicate names.

3. **Error diagnosis:** The system is capable to diagnose errors in student solutions accurately. For this purpose, it must be able to evaluate hypotheses about different possible solution variants created by students, i.e. the student's intended solution strategy underlying a solution must be determined and the implementation variant has to be hypothesized correctly.

4. **Ranking feedback's severity:** Feedback messages should be ranked according to the severity of underlying errors (e.g., severe errors are shown first) in order to give students an idea about the issues considered most important and the error to be removed solved first.

5. **Technical Aspects:** Since the system is intended to be used to support students solving homework exercises, it should be accessible from home, and thus it should be implemented as a web-based system.

3.3 Conceptual Design

In order to fulfil the first requirement of a tutoring system for logic programming, we propose a two-stage coaching strategy (Section 3.4). This tutoring model is intended to coach students during the task analysis and the implementation phase of a programming process.

To satisfy the second requirement, we focus on programming problems of the complexity level three according the classification of problems described in Section 2.4. From the perspective of ITS development and tutoring programming, this class of programming problems seems to be most attractive, because at this level of ambition programming is less focused on technical foundations, rather starts to develop into a real problem solving activity. The programming problem *Investment*, for instance, is an appropriate exercise assignment to be used in a tutoring system for programming, because it is complex and challenging enough both for the student to solve and for the system to diagnose errors. The students are required to have a range of knowledge of basic concepts including recursion, unification, arithmetic test, term test, and arithmetic calculation. Such a problem is a typical homework assignment given to students in the second part of a three-month curriculum of the logic programming course running at the Department of Informatics, University of Hamburg.

The third and the fourth requirements for a tutoring system in the domain of logic programming can be realised using the concepts of *weighted constraints* (Section 3.5) and *semantic table* (Section 3.6 and 3.7). Constraints and semantic table are used to span a large solution space for each programming problem. In addition, transformation rules which transform arithmetic expressions or a certain class of programs can be exploited to further extend the solution space. Constraint weights serve to control the process of error diagnosis. Furthermore, constraint weights can be used to decide on the most plausible hypothesis about the student's solution strategy underlying her solution and to rank the feedback messages according to the severity of errors.

The fifth requirement can be fulfilled using web technology and is described in Chapter 4. In the following subsequent sections, the concepts we propose to build a tutoring system for logic programming are elaborated in more details.

3.4 A Two-Stage Coaching Model

3.4.1 A Preliminary Study

A preliminary study has been conducted during the winter term 2004/05 at the University of Hamburg. The goal of this study was to evaluate the capability of a diagnostic component, to collect student programs, to identify the difficulties of the students while solving logic programming problems, and to determine where in the process of programming they are usually stuck. Students of the logic programming course have been invited to consult a web-based system when experiencing difficulties in solving their homework assignments. This system was a former version of INCOM and consisted of mainly a diagnostic component, which was able to identify errors in a few logic programs. The system attempted to diagnose errors in student solutions and returned diagnostic information based on which students should be able to improve their solution successively. The system provided students with four exercise assignments:

1. Define a predicate which specifies the relationship between a list and its prefix.
2. Write a function to convert Peano numbers to integer numbers.
3. Write a predicate which defines an even Peano number.
4. Write a function to compute the sum of compound interest for a given amount, an interest rate and a duration in years.

Totally, 261 log files which have been created by 99 users were collected. Each log file contained records of interactions of a user using the system to solve a task on one day. That is, if a user was engaged with the same task many times a day, the system created only one log file.

By analysing the log files, errors were collected and assigned according to the phases of the process of programming: 1) task analysis, 2) solution design and 3) implementation. The columns *Analysis, Design* and *Impl.* of Table 3.1 show the proportion of false attempts during the corresponding programming phases. The second column indicates the absolute number of false and total attempts to solve the tasks. The proportion of syntax errors is not reported because we only investigated the semantic correctness of a solution.

Although the error rate on the implementation phase was highest for Task 1 (54.9%), 2 (51.4%), and 4 (46.8%), the error rates of the task analysis and solution design phase were also remarkably high, e.g., students made 70% of errors in the phase of analysing Task 3, indicating that students mainly had difficulties in specifying the clause head for a predicate definition for Peano numbers correctly; 42% of students' attempts for Task 4 were not successful at finding appropriate clauses or subgoals. This result reveals the need for a coaching approach which is able to provide specific help corresponding to the phases of the process of programming.

Table 3.1: Error rate in the programming phases

Task	False/Total Attempts	Analysis	Design	Impl.
1	70/91	7%	20%	54.9 %
2	205/242	25%	18%	51.4%
3	210/246	70%	17%	8.9%
4	147/149	9%	42%	46.8%

The result of the previous study points out students' difficulties not only during the implementation phase of the process of programming, but also during the phases of task analysis and solution design. Therefore, students need appropriate feedback which matches the activity of the programming phase they are currently engaged in. The following example illustrates the problem of providing students with inappropriate feedback. The third exercise assignment of the previous study requests the students to define a predicate which tests whether a Peano number is even. A student submitted the following solution.

peano_even(Peano).
peano(Peano, Number):-peano(s(X)+2).

For this problem, the system expected a correct solution, e.g., like the following:

peano_even(0).
peano_even(s(s(X))):-peano_even(X).

The student implemented two predicates: *peano_even/1* and *peano/2*. Since the number of argument positions of the latter one did not meet the requirements of the problem, the system assumed that *peano_even/1* was intended to solve it. The system returned the corresponding diagnostic information:

3.4. A TWO-STAGE COACHING MODEL

Error 1 A base case (2. Clause) is superfluous.

Error 2 A recursive case is missing.

Error 3 The first argument position in the base case (1. Clause) should be 0.

We can guess that the student intended to implement the second clause as a recursive case for the predicate *peano_even/1*, but maybe she mistyped the name of the predicate. In addition, we notice that the second clause specifies a predicate which has two argument positions *Peano*, *Number*, but none of them has been used in the clause body. Hence, we could assume that she was not sure about how many argument positions are needed to solve the given problem. That means, she was not able to fully analyse the task. Therefore, feedback concerning solution design (Error 1 and 2) and implementation (Error 3) are not helpful for the student in this case. Instead, we need to help the student to properly analyse the task requirement. This is the motivation for us to develop a coaching strategy which helps students during the different phases of the process of programming. The goal is to provide appropriate feedback on different programming phases.

This thesis proposes a coaching model which consists of two stages. On the first stage, the students are requested to analyse a given programming task. Once they provide an appropriate result of their task analysis, they enter the second stage which focuses on the implementation. This two-stage coaching model does not include a separate stage for designing solutions. We assume that design activities can also be included in the second coaching stage and design skills can be acquired by providing feedback in terms of high level programming concepts, e.g., logic programming techniques. We focus on the task analysis and implementation phases of the programming process because these activities are considered two key issues of programming (Jeffries et al., 1981; Guzdial et al., 1998): 1) The decomposition problem is to identify the goal and information needed to solve the programming task; 2) The composition problem is to put the components (e.g., programming plans, schemata or other high-level programming concepts) together so that the programming task is solved correctly. Furthermore, Table 2.2 (cf. Section 2.5) reveals that the majority of existing systems for programming does not distinctly address the task analysis phase during programming, rather they tend to support implementation activities. The proposal of a two-stage coaching model in this thesis is meant to fill this gap.

The proposed two-stage coaching approach allows the student to iteratively refine a predicate signature and an implementation during each stage. From the point of view of software engineering, however, it resembles the water fall model which has been criticized as being impractical and not realistic. However, in a first attempt a trade-off between the didactic advantages and the real practice of programming has to be found.

From a didactic point of view, the appeal for coaching distinct phases of programming is supported by the findings of previous research which investigated typical behaviours of programming learners. First, several studies have shown that the first step most novice programmers carry out when writing a program is typing in code (Pintrich et al., 1987; Wender et al., 1987), and especially, they tend to deal with syntactic aspects of a programming language primarily (Pennington, 1987). Often, they analyse a task and design a solution in the middle of the coding process (Perkins et al., 1989, p. 257). This phenomenon might be explained by two hypotheses. First, we assume the student understands a problem expressed in a natural language, but she is not able to identify the information or goals given in the problem description which are initial keys to start coding a program. Second, even if the student is able to identify important information given in the problem description, she does not know how to "translate" it into expressions of a specific programming language. Thus, it is necessary to train novice programmers on how to carry out task analysis successfully.

A second typical behaviour displayed by many programming learners is using program output artifacts as a means to assess program quality (Joni and Soloway, 1986). They repeatedly change minor things in their program in the hope that changes might produce the desired program output. This kind of behaviour is usually accounted to poor planning. Hence, coaching students on different phases would motivate them to pursue a more systematic approach.

Furthermore, since programming is a complex problem solving activity, and the branching factor for non-trivial design tasks can be quite large (Soloway et al., 1988), a great number of decisions, that need to be taken, can make programming difficult for the learner. As a result, most programs are erroneous, because learners have to focus on many issues at a time, e.g., understanding the given problem, designing a solution, applying the syntax of a new programming language. According to the cognitive load theory, such a situation is not beneficial for learning if too many new topics are addressed at once, learning is hindered (Sweller, 1994). Therefore, supporting distinct phases would reduce the cognitive load of the student, because students are forced to only concentrate on necessary activities of each specific programming phase.

Some attempts have been made to coach students during different phases of the programming process (cf. Section 2.5). The LISP-Tutor supported students in the design and implementation phases, whereas the PROPL system focused on the task ana-lysis and design phases of the process of programming. Finally, the system BRIDGE (Bonar and Cunningham, 1988) was intended to guide a programming learner through the phases of task analysis, design and implementation. Unfortunately, the literature provides no information about a formal

3.4. A TWO-STAGE COACHING MODEL

evaluation.

3.4.2 Task Analysis

Task analysis aims at establishing an understanding of the given problem and developing a mental representation of the task (Lane, 2004). To help students to understand a given problem, BRIDGE (Bonar and Cunningham, 1988) guides them to identify and refine the goals for the code by selecting simple patterns of natural language phrases. Similarly, PROPL coaches students to understand a given problem by holding a conversation. The system asks questions about the information in the problem statement and allows students to answer them using unrestricted natural language. For this purpose, the author of PROPL studied conversations between human tutors and students during numerous tutoring sessions and identified common communication patterns. Using natural language to conduct a conversation between students and the system as they do with human tutors is one of the strengths of PROPL. However, this approach suffers from the limited completeness of the database of communication patterns.

As an alternative, this thesis proposes to help students to understand a programming problem by requesting them to reproduce information and goals given in the problem description in form of an adequate predicate signature which consists of the following components:

- A *predicate_name* which is the identifier of the predicate to be implemented;
- Argument names which serve as unique identifiers for the argument positions of the predicate;
- *Meaning(A_i)* represents the purpose of the argument position A_i. This kind of information is selected by identifying an appropriate concept used in the problem description;
- *Type(A_i)* represents the data structure for the argument position A_i. Actually, logic programming does not require to specify data types for variables, the computation is based on unification techniques. However, from a pedagogical point of view, it might be useful to request the student to specify the data structure she intends to use at the particular argument position. Most frequently used data structures in logic programming are *atom*, *list* and *number*. Apart from these data structures, other terms can be classified as *arbitrary type*;
- *Mode(A_i)* is the calling mode for the argument position A_i. For a given predicate whose number of argument position is greater than 0, each argument position can be specified to be in one of three calling modes: Input (+), output (-) or indeterminate (?).

Prolog experts recommend learners to comment their code in order to indicate a predicate's intended usage. The predicate signature above is consistent with the annotation found in many

Prolog libraries[2] (Brna, 2001), e.g., SWI-Prolog.

Specifying a predicate signature in this way, the student is free to place the position of each argument and to name the identifiers according to her understanding of a given problem. As long as the signature input from the student is not yet appropriate with respect to the problem, the student is advised by the system on how to extract important information and goals from the problem description.

Often, problem statements may indicate explicit information and goals which can be identified immediately. However, sometimes information can also be hidden in a problem statement and cannot be identified directly. For example, the problem statement "Write a predicate which reverses the order of the elements of a *list*" contains the noun *"list"* which can be used to model an argument position which has the data structure "list". To implement this predicate we need a second argument position which represents the output of a reversed list. Unfortunately, no such information is indicated explicitly in the problem description for the second required argument position. In such a case, it is necessary to elicit information hidden in a problem statement to help the student specify an appropriate predicate signature. One approach is that the exercise author should revise the problem statement so that the nouns, which should be used to represent required argument positions, occur in the problem statement.

Under the assumption that the students are able to derive a proper understanding from the natural language problem description, we suggest to provide feedback by highlighting important noun phrases in the problem statement and to give the student hints on how to elicit information from the highlighted terms. This feature seems to be advantageous from a pedagogical point of view. The student is requested to read the problem text thoroughly and to think about highlighted noun phrases in the problem description. She is left to reason about the required information communicated by them. This kind of feedback may not be as helpful as the one produced by BRIDGE and PROPL. These systems establish a dialogue with the student, e.g., asking about the kind of information the student can identify in the problem description. Building a natural language dialogue system, however, is not the focus of this thesis.

The approach of supporting students in analysing a problem by specifying a predicate signature still has several limitations. First, this coaching approach is not able to cover all possible understanding problems. For instance, if the student did not know the concept of Peano numbers, then coaching her to specify a predicate signature for a task of checking whether a Peano number is even would not help her further. This kind of knowledge should have been

---

[2]In standard libraries, the component *Meaning(A_i)*, which conceives the purpose of each argument position, is normally represented in free-text natural language which, however, cannot easily be understood by a software system.

3.4. A TWO-STAGE COACHING MODEL

acquired during lectures or from text books but not on the stage of task analysis. Second, the requirement to specify noun phrases for the argument positions of a predicate signature explicitly, might easily render the task description look artificially. For example, most exercise descriptions do not include the noun phrase which represents the result of a computation, like for the problem of reversing a list mentioned above. An approach which could help students to think about hidden information (e.g., the nouns representing argument positions, or the data structure of an argument position) is desired. Third, it is not always possible to derive a unique data type for an argument position from a noun phrase if the noun phrase does not indicates a data type explicitly. For example, a noun phrase like "A pair of persons" does not point to a specific data type. Therefore, various data types can be used: e.g., a list [A,B], a predicate relation p(A,B), or two argument positions can be used to represent two persons A and B. In such a case, if the student is forced to use the predicate signature exactly as specified by the exercise author, this will narrow down the space of solution variability considerably. Despite of these limitations, there are reasons to believe that analysing a programming problem by specifying a signature prior to the implementation is a good programming practice. From a pedagogical point of view, guiding the student to focus on the implementation once she has finished the task analysis phase helps her not to stray away from the implementation goal. From a technical point of view, the task analysis stage not only encourages the student to practice analysing tasks, but also provides valuable information which helps to make the subsequent error diagnosis more accurate. We will discuss the issue of error diagnosis in Section 3.8.

Once the student has provided an appropriate signature, which satisfies the given problem, the system guides her to the second stage where she is allowed to design and implement a program.

3.4.3 Implementation

If the student has specified an appropriate predicate signature, she is guided to the second stage where she is asked to implement a predicate for a given problem by taking the specified predicate signature into account. Therefore, the information about the agreed upon predicate signature is displayed:

1. $predicate\_name(Mode(A_1)Type(A_1),\ Mode(A_2)Type(A_2),\ ...)$
2. $predicate\_name(Meaning(A_1),\ Meaning(A_2),\ ...)$

A predicate is implemented by defining clauses. To be able to follow the intention of the student, for each clause, the system asks her to additionally specify the type of the clause she intends to implement. In logic programming clauses can be classified into three types:

recursive case, *base case*, and *non-recursive*. Recursive cases are clauses which compute an argument recursively. Base cases represent clauses which define the conditions under which a recursion terminates. Clauses of other types can be assigned to the non-recursive cases.

If necessary, the student can revise the specified predicate signature, e.g., by changing the order of the argument positions. Furthermore, if she needs to define a helper predicate or an accumulative predicate (if the problem can be solved accumulatively), she also can use the option to specify an additional signature for the new helper predicate. If the student implementation, including the main predicate and the helper predicate, does not fulfil the goals specified in the given problem, the system provides feedback to improve the implementation. We will discuss feedback types in Section 3.9.

3.5 Modelling Programming Knowledge

3.5.1 A Constraint-based Model

In order to coach the student at both stages, helpful feedback about the shortcomings of her solution[3] is desired. Hence, the solution is subjected to a thorough diagnosis. In this thesis, constraints are the basis for the process of diagnosing errors.

The basic idea of constraint-based diagnosis is building a model which represents the space of correct solutions and checking whether a solution is licensed by this model. The constraint representation described in Section 2.6.4 can be used to model different types of knowledge.

First, whenever a given problem domain is characterized by certain principles, they can be modelled by means of *general constraints* according to the following schema:

Type **(1)**
    IF   problem situation X is relevant
  THEN condition Y must be satisfied

where the problem situation X and the condition Y can be composed of many elementary propositions using conjunction or disjunction operators.

Second, constraints can be used to model specific properties of correct solutions. If a solution violates a constraint, the solution does not satisfy a semantic requirement of correct solutions. This way of using constraints as the only means to model correct solutions has been proposed by Ohlsson (1994), but it comes with two disadvantages (cf. Section 2.6.4): constraints may become very complex and are problem-specific. An alternative approach is using an *ideal solution* to capture the semantic correctness required to solve a given problem and constraints are used to establish the relationship between the student solution and the

---

[3]The term *solution* is used in general. It can be a predicate signature or an implementation.

3.5. MODELLING PROGRAMMING KNOWLEDGE

specified ideal solution (Mitrovic et al., 2007). The ideal solution then defines the canonical solution strategy the student has to follow. Thus, a constraint-based tutor which uses an ideal solution to check student solutions might provide misleading feedback, if the student follows an alternative solution strategy not corresponding to the one underlying the ideal solution (cf. Section 2.6.4). To address this issue, Martin (2001) suggested building a problem solver which constructs (partial) correct solutions following the same solution strategy as the one of the student solution. This technique has been applied successfully in the domain of SQL, but building a problem solver is not an easy task for all domains (Mitrovic et al., 2001, p. 932). To address this problem, the thesis adopts a so-called *semantic table* which represents information required by correct solutions to a problem. The concept of semantic table comprises two ideas: 1) it captures several solution strategies, and 2) it represents model solutions in a generalised form which is able to cover implementation variants created by alternative orderings of program statements (cf. Section 3.1.2). The relational representation of semantic correctness of a solution has the advantage that information from the table can be accessed directly without parsing the model solution. The semantic table can be instantiated in two ways: *signature table* and *implementation table*. The first one is used to diagnose errors in a predicate signature, and the second serves to diagnose errors in an implementation. How each type of semantic table is defined and how its information can be accessed, will be demonstrated later in the specific case of error diagnosis. The constraints, which use information from the semantic table to check the semantic correctness of the student solution, are called *semantic constraints* and have the following general form:

 Type **(2)**
  IF in the semantic table, a component X exists and satisfies condition α
  THEN in the student solution, a corresponding component must exist and satisfy
    condition α

Constraint schema Type (2) can be specialized further to check for missing or superfluous components in the student solution (Type (2.1) and (2.2)) or to check whether a component in the student solution has a required property (Type (2.3)).

 Type **(2.1)**
  IF in the semantic table, a component X exists
  THEN in the student solution, a component corresponding to X must also exist

 Type **(2.2)**
  IF in the student solution, a component Y exists
  THEN in the semantic table, a component corresponding to Y must also exist

Type **(2.3)**
  IF in the semantic table, a component Z exists and has property A
  THEN in the student solution, a component corresponding to Z must also exist and have property A

3.5.2 A Formalism For Weighted Constraints

Constraint-based error diagnosis can be conceived as a constraint satisfaction problem. If a student solution is correct, then all constraints will be satisfied. If an erroneous student solution is evaluated, an inconsistency between the erroneous student solution and the constraint system occurs, i.e., several constraints will be violated. In this case, the problem of error diagnosis is considered over-constrained. The goal of constraint-based error diagnosis is not to search a correct solution, rather to identify the constraint violations which lead to the inconsistency between an erroneous solution and the constraint system.

To deal with the issue of over-constrained satisfaction problems, researchers attempt to distinguish the level of importance between constraints, e.g, *hard constraints* represent conditions which must always be hold and *soft constraints* represent preferences which should be satisfied when possible. Several techniques have been devised to express soft constraints and to allow them being violated. The most popular approaches include fuzzy constraint satisfaction problems (CSPs) (Dubois et al., 1996), cost-minimizing CSPs[4] (Schiex et al., 1995), partial CSPs (Freuder and Wallace, 1992), and probabilistic CSPs (Fargier and Lang, 1993).

A partial CSPs framework attempts to soft a constraint satisfaction problem by changing the domain of variables/constraints or a constraint system in several ways: 1) enlarging the domain of a variable, 2) by enlarging the domain of a constraint, 3) by removing variables of a constraint, or 4) by removing a constraint from the constraint system. This approach is not appropriate to enhance the capability of constraint-based error diagnosis of a CBM tutoring system due to the following reason. To choose the most plausible solution strategy we need to consider all possible evidences (based on used programming constructs), whereas a partial CSPs framework attempts to eliminate constraints which can be violated by a student solution and thus, evidences supporting the process of hypothesizing the student's intention during error diagnosis are also eliminated. As a consequence, the diagnosis capability of a CBM tutoring system would be degraded.

Whereas a partial CSPs framework requires to satisfy a partial set of constraints, the fuzzy

---

[4]In the literature, researchers refer to this kind of problems as *weighted* constraint satisfaction problems. We avoid to use this notion because we will use the term *weighted constraint* to describe the importance of a constraint later.

3.5. MODELLING PROGRAMMING KNOWLEDGE

CSPs and the cost-minimizing CSPs approaches allow all constraints to be satisfied by defining a preference ranking of the possible instantiations according to some criteria depending on the constraints and the solution of a fuzzy/ cost-minimizing constraint satisfaction problem is the one which meets the highest satisfaction degree. While the fuzzy CSPs framework associates a level of preference with each instantiation of variables in each constraint, in a cost-minimizing CSP framework instantiations are assigned with a cost. A fuzzy CSP framework searches a solution by maximizing the satisfaction degree of the least preferred constraint. The goal of a cost-minimizing CSP framework is to find a solution which minimizes the total sum of costs of the chosen instantiation for each constraint. These approaches are best suited to problem situations where preference levels for certain instantiations of the constraint variables are available. These approaches are not appropriate to enhance the capability of constraint-based error diagnosis due to two reasons. First, the problem of error diagnosis in a CBM tutoring system is a situation where it is almost impossible to specify instantiations of constraint variables in advance because the amount of constraints required to model domain knowledge is relatively high and the space of possible instantiations is large. Second, fuzzy CSPs and cost-minimizing frameworks normally require that the set of constraint variables of the problem is known in advance. In the case of diagnosing a program, the mapping between the components of a student solution and a set of constraint variables is not unique, i.e., several components of the student solution may be associated to the same constraint variable, and thus, constraints cannot be evaluated.

A probabilistic CSPs framework, finally, contains a set of constraints, each of them is associated with a probability of relevance. That is, some constraints are relevant to the real problem with a complete certainty, and some others may or may not be relevant to a problem. It is assumed that the probabilities of two different constraints are independent from each other because each constraint is intended to represent a piece of knowledge. A solution of the probabilistic constraint satisfaction problem is an instantiation of all variables which has the highest probability. A probabilistic CSPs framework can be used to model situations where each constraint can be specified with a certain probability. Since such a situation is applicable to the domain of logic programming, this thesis adopts the probabilistic approach to enhance the diagnosis capability of traditional CBM tutoring systems. In the approach pursued here, a probability associated with each constraint indicates a measure of the importance of a constraint and being referred to as a *constraint weight*. By applying the probabilistic CSPs approach, the determination of importance level for constraints resembles the correction of written examinations by a human tutor: if a student solution contains more important components, then it receives a better mark. The primary goal of using constraint weights is to choose the most plausible hypothesis about the solution variant submitted by the student during the process of error diagnosis.

To find a solution for a probabilistic constraint satisfaction problem, which is a complete instantiation of variables, researchers usually propose a multiplicative model (Fargier and Lang, 1993; Shazeer et al., 1999). That is, the probability of a solution is computed by taking the constraints violated by that solution into account and multiplying their weights. The solution which has the highest probability is considered the most probable one. Similarly, following the goal of searching the most plausible hypothesis about the student's solution variant, we need to evaluate the plausibility of all possible hypotheses. For this purpose, we also apply a multiplicative model. Constraint weights are suggested to be taken from the interval $[0;1]$, where a value close to 1 represents the weight for least important constraints and 0 indicates the weight for constraints which model the most important requirements. The constraints of the latter type can be considered hard constraints. If a hard constraint is violated, the plausibility score becomes 0, and we know that an important requirement has not been satisfied. The importance of a constraint is determined based on the role of the components being investigated. Constraints checking a component which contributes more information to the overall correctness of the solution should receive a weight value tending to the value 0. Constraint weight values need to be adjusted manually to yield acceptable diagnostic results.

Another way to calculate the plausibility score would be to add up the weights of all constraint violations. However, applying such an additive model does not allow us to trace whether hard constraint violations have contributed to the plausibility score.

As discussed in Section 2.6.4, constraints, which are solely based on a binary logic (violated or not), do not contain sufficient information to decide on the most plausible hypothesis about the solution strategy implemented in the student solution. A simple approach to compare different hypotheses is to count the number of constraints which are violated by each hypothesis (Menzel, 1992). However, this kind of measure is too gross and may result in inaccurate diagnostic information. On the course of diagnosing errors, the secondary goal of using constraint weights is to determine the most plausible solution strategy underlying the student solution. In addition to the goals of diagnosing errors and determining the most plausible strategy underlying the student solution, constraint weights can serve to prioritize feedback messages which explain errors occurred in the student solution. Hence, the use of constraint weights meet the third and the fourth requirement for the coaching system for logic programming (cf. Section 3.2).

With the inclusion of constraint weights, the representation of a weighted constraint specified in a CBM tutoring system consists of the following components:

3.6. MODELLING THE SPACE OF PREDICATE SIGNATURES

1. ID: An unique identification name of a constraint. The constraint ID is used as a reference to control the diagnosis process.
2. Relevance (IF): Conditions under which the constraint is relevant.
3. Satisfaction (THEN): Conditions which a correct solution has to satisfy.
4. Weight: The importance of the constraint.
5. Hint: The error explanation to be displayed in case the constraint is violated.

3.6 Modelling The Space of Predicate Signatures

A predicate signature is composed of a predicate name and a set of argument positions, each of them consists of its meaning, a data type and a calling mode (Figure 3.3). The structural hierarchy of a predicate signature includes two levels: Predicate name and argument positions on the first level; The argument's meaning, the data type and the calling mode on the second one.

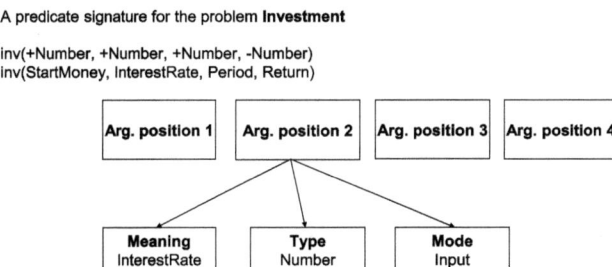

Figure 3.3: The structural hierarchy of a predicate signature.

A constraint-based model for a predicate signature can be built applying the constraint schemas described in the preceding section to the components of the predicate signature. For example, the constraint schema Type (1) can be used to define a constraint D1 which requires that the name of the predicate being specified is different from the built-in predicates.

    ID   **D1**
    IF   a predicate name is N
  THEN N must be different from the name of built-in predicates
WEIGHT 0.1
  HINT It is not allowed to redefine a built-in predicate.

Contrary to general constraints, which solely operate on the student solution, semantic constraints establish an interaction with a semantic table. Requirements for the components of

Table 3.2: A signature table for the problem *Investment*

Predicate	Arg. Position	Meaning	Type	Mode
p	Arg1	"Start Money"	number	+
p	Arg2	"Interest rate"	number	+
p	Arg3	"Investment period"	number	+
p	Arg4	"Return on investment"	number	-

a predicate signature are modelled in the *signature table*. Each entry of the table consists of a 5-tuple ⟨predicate name, argument name, meaning, data type, calling mode⟩. The first two columns of the table represent the identifiers for a predicate and for an argument position. They are mapped to the corresponding predicate's identifier and argument positions of the student's predicate signature. It is not required that the identifiers in the student's predicate signature have to be the same as the ones specified in the semantic table. The column representing the meaning of an argument position contains a list of possible relevant concepts which occur in the problem description and might be used to describe that argument position. An argument's data type and calling mode are selected from a list of possible values (e.g., an argument's data type can be either an atom, a list, a number or an arbitrary data structure) according to the meaning of the argument position. This way, a semantic table of this type covers the space of possible predicate signatures which may have different order of the argument positions or identifier names.

A signature table for the problem *Investment* can be represented by Table 3.2, which shows that a predicate to be implemented needs four argument positions. They represent the initial investment sum, the yearly interest rate, the investment period, and the return on investment. The first three argument positions are of input mode and the last one is of output mode. Using information in the signature table, constraint schema Type (2.3) can be instantiated to specify constraint D2 which checks the type of an argument position.

    ID **D2**
    IF in the signature table, the argument position represents meaning concept X has type *atom*
  THEN in the student's predicate signature, an argument position corresponding to X is specified with type *atom*
WEIGHT 0.3
  HINT The mode specified for this argument position does not correspond to the problem description.

The constraints (both semantic and general) which are defined for this stage of coaching are

3.7. MODELLING THE SPACE OF IMPLEMENTATIONS

called *declaration constraints*. With respect to specifying the weight value for declaration constraints, the predicate name and the argument positions are the most important components of the predicate signature, and thus have a constraint weight close to the value 0. The components within an argument position (the argument's meaning, the data type and the calling mode) are less important, because they belong to a lower level of the structural hierarchy. Therefore, they should be specified with a weight closer to the value 1. For example, we have chosen the weight value 0.1 for constraint D1 which is defined to examine whether the student has reused the predicate name of a built-in predicate. Constraint D2, checking the mode of an argument position, is weighted as being less important (0.3).

3.7 Modelling The Space of Implementations

To diagnose errors in the implementation, a tutoring system must be able to cover the space of possible implementations for a programming problem and to identify the reason why a solution does not belong to that space. In this section, we attempt to achieve the first goal.

In Section 2.3 we have distinguished two levels of solution variability: solution strategy and implementation. On the implementation level, the factors which determine the solution space for a programming problem are: 1) the existence of syntactic reformulations, 2) the possibility of reordering the sequence of programming constructs, 3) the option of naming identifiers, and 4) the possibility of defining new helper predicates.

We apply the concept of the semantic table and weighted constraints (cf. Section 3.5) to model the space of implementations for a logic programming problem. An *implementation table* is specified to represent alternative solution strategies for a given problem description. A matching process matches the student implementation against components of each solution strategy described in the implementation table and results in mappings. Thus, identifier names do not play a role in the process of error diagnosis because the object underlying an identifier name can be identified by means of these mappings. Constraints are used to check the semantic correctness as well as the well-formedness of the implementation based on the resulting mappings. Furthermore, transformation rules are used to cover a large space of semantically equivalent variants of arithmetic expressions and helper predicates.

3.7.1 An Implementation Table

The hierarchy of a Prolog predicate consists of the following components: clause, clause head, subgoal, functor and argument. For arithmetic expressions, the hierarchy includes multiplication term, algebraic sign and product factor.

Since the implementation table is used to represent the relationship between components of a predicate, the hierarchy of the predicate is flattened so that each entry of the table includes all components of a predicate. In addition, since alternative solution strategies may exist, each entry must also indicate the solution strategy explicitly. Hence, each entry of the table consists of a tuple representing the relational relationship between the following components: a solution strategy, a clause head and a subgoal.

To model a possible solution strategy for a problem, a unique identifier is specified in the column *solution strategy*. The required components of the solution strategy are modelled in the columns *clause head, subgoal* of the table. Several table entries with the same solution strategy identifier build a *generalised solution description* (GSD) which represents the semantic requirements of each solution strategy. Since the relational representation allows us to access clauses and associated subgoals directly, these components are not restricted to a particular sequential ordering. Thus, *the implementation table serves two modelling purposes: 1) alternative solution strategies and 2) alternative sequential orderings*. However, if the sequential ordering of the subgoals has to be restricted (e.g., in case of an arithmetic test or a calculation subgoal), then the order of the entries must be specified accordingly i.e., the subgoal which has to precede another one on the sequence needs to be specified with a lower index value. Clause head and subgoals are represented in a *normal form* according to the following rules:

- A clause head must be of the form: $p(x_1, ..., x_n)$ where $x_1, ..., x_n$ must be variables.
- All variables of the clause head must be distinct, that is $x_i \neq x_j$ $(i \neq j)$.
- An arithmetic expression is represented as a sum of multiplication terms without nested expressions.

To specify a clause in the semantic table, according to these rules, unification between the arguments of the clause head or (de)composition at an argument position must be made explicit by means of a subgoal. The dependencies between the arguments are represented implicitly by co-reference requirements between these subgoals. Thus, the normal form representation has the benefit that it reveals the underlying programming techniques, e.g., unification.

For example, Table 3.3[5] shows the generalised solution descriptions of the four solution strategies which can be applied to solve the problem *Investment*, where the column *Description* serves to explain the necessity of each subgoal. The fourth part of this table, for instance, describes the required semantics to implement the solution strategy *recursive and arithmetic_after*. It requires two clauses: a base case and a recursive case. The recursive clause requires the existence of a recursive subgoal for a new period, an update for a new investment period, and a calculation of the aggregated return of investment.

---

[5]This table serves as illustration. In reality, it contains no redundant data.

3.7. MODELLING THE SPACE OF IMPLEMENTATIONS

Table 3.3: An implementation table for the problem *Investment*

Str.	CI	Head	SI	Subgoal	Description
1	1	p(S,R,P,Ret)	1	Ret is $S*(R+1)\hat{\ }P$	Using a formula
2	1	p(S,_,P,Ret)	1	P=0	Recursion stops
2	1	p(S,_,P,Ret)	2	Ret=S	Return equal start money
2	2	p(S,R,P,Ret)	1	P>0	Check period
2	2	p(S,R,P,Ret)	2	NS is S*R+S	Calculate new sum
2	2	p(S,R,P,Ret)	3	NP is P-1	Update period
2	2	p(S,R,P,Ret)	4	p(NS,R,NP,Ret)	Recur with new period
3	1	p(S,_,P,S)	1	P=0	Recursion stops
3	2	p(S,R,P,Ret)	1	$P > 0$	Check period
3	2	p(S,R,P,Ret)	2	NP is P-1	Update period
3	2	p(S,R,P,Ret)	3	p(S,R,NP,NS)	Recur with new period
3	2	p(S,R,P,Ret)	4	Ret is NS + R*NS	Calculate return
4	1	p(S,_,P,S)	1	P=0	Recursion stops
4	2	p(S,R,P,Ret)	1	p(S,R,NP,NE)	Invest. of remaining period
4	2	p(S,R,P,Ret)	2	P is NP+1	Update remaining period
4	2	p(S,R,P,Ret)	3	Ret is NE+R*NE	Calculate return

Str. 1: analytic strategy; Str. 2: tail recursive strategy; Str. 3: recursive and arithmetic_before strategy; Str. 4: recursive and arithmetic_after strategy; CI: clause index; SI: subgoal index

Representing semantic requirements of solution strategies using the concept of the semantic table is more advantageous in comparison to the approach of using an ideal solution. First, the semantic table can cover alternative solution strategies for a problem whereas an ideal solution represents only a single solution strategy. Second, information about the required components for the implementation of a solution strategy can be easily accessed by an appropriate query, whereas an ideal solution needs to be decomposed first before it can be used. Thereby, the diagnosis becomes more adequate on the conceptual level and the resulting feedback is more useful. However, a semantic table can only be specified with a limited number of different solution strategies for a programming problem.

3.7.2 Weighted Constraints

We apply the constraint schemata to define constraints to span the space of correct implementations for a logic programming problem. All constraints defined for the purpose of modelling a space of implementations are referred to as *implementation constraints*. They are divided into the following types:

General Constraints

First, applying the constraint schema Type (1) we are able specify general constraints which express general semantic principles of the programming language. They are not specific to any task and must be satisfied by any correct implementation. Ge-neral principles of this kind are, for instance, the existence requirements of base cases and recursive cases for a recursive implementation. Modelling this principle as a ge-neral constraint (G1[6]), the problem situation, which will be specified in the relevance part of the constraint, is implementing a recursive predicate, and the condition which must be satisfied is the existence of at least a base case and a recursive case.

> ID **G1**
> IF The student indicates (by entering an appropriate clause type) that predicate p is intended to implement a recursion
> THEN There exists at least a base case and a recursive case
> HINT A base case or a recursive case is missing.

Since constraint G1 is formulated in natural language in order to provide a comfortable understanding, it looks simple. Internally, it is very complex and this has a major impact on the accuracy of diagnostic results (as discussed in Section 2.6.4). Thus, constraint G1 can be broken down into two constraints: one checks the existence of base cases (G1.1), and another one for recursive cases. This has the advantage that feedback becomes more accurate because the diagnostic result indicates precisely whether the existence of base cases or recursive cases is the reason of the error.

> ID **G1.1**
> IF The predicate p is intended to implement a recursion
> THEN There exists at least a base case
> HINT A base case is missing.

In addition to checking the semantic correctness of an implementation on the basis of structural components, the instantiation of an argument position contributes to the semantics of a predicate (Vasconcelos, 1995). The instantiation state of an argument can be obtained starting from the already specified predicate signature (cf. Section 3.4.2). It determines the calling mode of argument positions, which then are propagated into all argument positions within the clause from left to right. An instantiation state of an argument is either "instantiated" or "free". Such information cannot be read off from the structure of a Prolog predicate definition

---

[6]We intend not to mention the constraint weight in the examples for constraints in this section, because we discuss the choice of the weight value in Section 3.7.2.

3.7. MODELLING THE SPACE OF IMPLEMENTATIONS

alone. The information about the instantiation state of each argument can be represented as a tuple of <argument position, argument value, instantiation state>, where *argument position* includes a clause index, a subgoal index and an argument index, and *argument value* indicates the term/variable representing that argument.

Constraint G2 is a general constraint which checks the instantiation state of arguments of an arithmetic test. The principle requires that two operands of an arithmetic test, e.g., X>Y, must have been instantiated to a value before they can be compared. Here, the problem situation is an arithmetic test between two arguments, and the satisfaction condition requires that the arguments must be instantiated.

    ID   **G2**
    IF X is a variable existing in an arithmetic test subgoal
  THEN X has the instantiation state *instantiated*
  HINT   The operands of an arithmetic test must be instantiated to be executable.

Pre-implementation Constraints

Pre-implementation constraints check whether an implementation is appropriate according to the information provided by the predicate signature and the specification of clause types. The constraint schema Type (1) can be instantiated to define pre-implementation constraints. For instance, the following constraint Pre1 checks the data type compatibility between the predicate signature specified by the student and her implementation. The relevance part of this constraint describes the problem situation of specifying an argument position in the implementation according to the information in the predicate signature, and the condition which is defined in the satisfaction part requires that the value of the argument position must correspond to the specification.

    ID   **Pre1**
    IF   In the student implementation, the value at the argument position X is of type $Type\_X$
           AND in the predicate signature which has been specified by the student, the data type of the argument position X is π
  THEN $Type\_X$ is identical to π
  HINT   You have specified π as a data type for the argument position X. Hence, the value of X should correspond to π.

Semantic Constraints

Semantic constraints can be defined applying the constraint schemata Type (2), (2.1), (2.2), and (2.3). For example, the following semantic constraint is defined to examine whether an arithmetic test subgoal (e.g., $X < 1$) specified in the GSD also exists in the student implementation:

    ID   **S1**
    IF   An arithmetic test subgoal $X \triangleleft Y$, which compares X with Y, is specified in the GSD
    THEN   A corresponding subgoal comparing a variable SX with SY exists in the student implementation
    HINT   In the clause body, a subgoal which tests SX with SY is missing.

Similarly, constraint schema Type (2.2) can be applied to define a constraint to check whether an arithmetic test subgoal is superfluous in the student implementation. Instances of constraint schema Type (2.3) can be used to examine the required property of a specific component. For example, the following constraint checks the required value of the operand of an arithmetic test.

    ID   **S2**
    IF   An arithmetic test $X \triangleleft Y$ is specified in the GSD
           AND Y has value N
           AND there exists a corresponding subgoal $SX \triangleleft SY$ in the student implementation
    THEN SY has value N
    HINT   The subgoal requires to compare SX with value N.

Similar semantic constraints for implementation are defined for all components of a logic program: clause, clause head, subgoal of different types (decomposition, recursion, calculation, arithmetic test, unification, term test and user-defined), argument and functor, and particular components of an arithmetic expression (multiplication term, algebraic sign and product factor).

To model syntactic reformulations, constraint schema Type (2) can be instantiated and the disjunctive connector (OR) is used to enumerate different possible variants of an implementation in the satisfaction part of a constraint. For example, constraint S3 checking the correctness of an arithmetic expression generalises across a range of arithmetic comparators $(>, <, >=, =<)$ and their commutative variants, where $\triangleleft_s$ is an arithmetic comparator in the student solution. For example, both cases X<1 and 1>X should satisfy that constraint:

3.7. MODELLING THE SPACE OF IMPLEMENTATIONS

    ID   **S3**
    IF   In the GSD, there exists an arithmetic test $X \triangleleft Y$
           AND $SX \triangleleft_s SY$ is a corresponding subgoal in the student implementation
THEN $\triangleleft_s$ is identical to $\triangleleft$, and SX, SY correspond to X, Y
           OR $\triangleleft_s = rev_o(\triangleleft)$, and SX, SY correspond to Y, X
 HINT   Either the operator $\triangleleft_s$ or the operand arguments are wrong.

Pattern Constraints

Pattern constraints model standard solution strategies. They are used to build hypotheses about the solution strategy implemented by the student, and to derive strategy-related feedback. Pattern constraints are partly redundant to semantic constraints, but can be used to enhance the explanatory quality of the diagnostic results. Hence, they are not mandatory. When specifying the solution strategy for each problem in the semantic table, a corresponding pattern name can be associated. However, not always a suitable pattern can be found for all possible exercise types and solution strategies because the solution strategy might be too specific for a certain problem and cannot be applied to solve common problems.

The pattern *Process-All-Elements* (cf. Section 3.1.3) has the property that a base case is required. This property can be represented by the pattern constraint **Process-All-Elements**. The relevance part of this constraint checks whether this pattern name is specified in the semantic table (if a pattern is available). The satisfaction part requires the existence of a base case in the student solution.

    ID   **Process-All-Elements**
    IF   The pattern *test_all_elements* is implemented
THEN   A base case must exist
 HINT   A recursion needs a base case to terminate.

Constraint Weight

The weight value for the implementation constraints is determined based on the importance of each component within a predicate. Given the fact that a clause contributes more information to the overall correctness of the solution than an argument or a functor, a constraint which examines an argument should be specified as being less important compared to a constraint considering a subgoal.

The pre-implementation constraints are considered most important because they require that the student must implement a predicate corresponding to her intention (in terms of the specification of the predicate signature and clause types). If one of the pre-implementation constraints is violated, it indicates a severe error. Therefore, we assign pre-implementation constraints with weight value 0.

Table 3.4 contains weight values which have been chosen for the constraints checking the implementation of a Prolog predicate.

Table 3.4: Used constraint weights

Constraint Weight	Checking Issues
0.00	Compatibility between implementation and intention
0.01	Clause existence
0.1	Subgoal existence
0.3	Correctness of comparison operators/operands
0.5	Argument existence, position, co-reference
0.7	Subgoal order, factors of a multiplication term

3.7.3 Transformation Rules

Arithmetic Expressions

A programming technique or a construct can be instantiated in many different ways. Especially, arithmetic expressions allow a great variety of equivalent formulations. In order to represent the space of alternatives in a general manner, transformation rules can be defined to cover the most important practical cases. We consider only arithmetic expressions according to Definition 3.1.5. Transformation rules produce semantically equivalent distributive and associative reformulations which then can be checked against the student solution.

- Rule 1 transforms the normal form to the simplified form applying the distributive law: $A \circ X \pm B \circ X \rightarrow (A \pm B) \circ X$ where the operator $\circ$ is either * or /. If A and B are numbers, then $(A \pm B) \circ X$ can be transformed to $M \circ X$ where $M = A \pm B$. For example: $(2+3) * X \rightarrow 5 * X$.
- Rule 2 transforms a product/additive term applying the commutative law: $A * B \rightarrow B * A$ and $A + B \rightarrow B + A$.

Helper predicates

As indicated in Section 3.1.2, there are two cases to define a helper predicate: 1) modularising a program for the purpose of reusing certain code, and 2) defining an accumulative predicate.

For the first case (for an example see Section 3.1.2), the transformation techniques unfolding/folding developed by Tamaki and Sato (1984) can be applied in order to embed the

3.8. ERROR DIAGNOSIS

implementation of the helper predicate into the main one. This results in a new predicate without a subgoal calling a helper predicate. Based on the transformed predicate, error diagnosis is executed as usual. However, the unfolding/folding transformation techniques cannot be applied to cases where both the helper and the main predicate are recursive ones. This restriction can be represented in form of an appropriate constraint. For the second case, we anticipate a helper predicate and specify it in the semantic table for diagnostic purposes.

We have shown in Section 3.6 and 3.7 that weighted constraints, the semantic table and transformation rules can be used to create a model which covers a large solution space for a logic programming problem. The option of introducing identifier names can be realised by matching the student solution against the information specified in the semantic table during the process of error diagnosis (cf. Section 3.8).

Table 3.5: Modelling techniques

Technique	is/are used to model
Signature table	predicate signatures
Implementation table	alternative solution strategies, alternative sequential orderings obligatory solution elements
Weighted constraints	syntactic reformulations
Transformation rules	helper predicates, syntactic reformulations of arithmetic expressions
Matching process	identifier names

Table 3.5 summarizes the purpose of the proposed modelling techniques. As a conclusion, our Hypothesis 1 that *it is possible to build a domain model that covers a large solution space for a logic programming problem using the representation of weighted constraints, semantic tables, and a set of transformation rules* has been confirmed.

3.8 Error Diagnosis

In the preceding sections, we did model a space of solutions for both coaching stages on the basis of weighted constraints. In this section, we use these models to diagnose errors in the student solutions.

Although a predicate signature and a predicate implementation have different structure, they have one characteristic in common, they can be constructed in many ways. Thus, the process of diagnosing errors in both types of solutions is based on the same principle: 1) generating hypotheses about possible variants of the student solution by matching components of the student solution against the corresponding ones in the semantic table and 2) evaluating hypotheses by checking the relevant constraints.

3.8.1 Hypothesis Generation

Since the components of a solution form a structural hierarchy with several levels, e.g., the structure of a Prolog predicate (cf. Figure 3.1) or the structure of a predicate signature (cf. Figure 3.3), hypotheses about a student solution can be generated subsequently on each level of the structural hierarchy.

Definition 3.8.1 *Let be G the set of n components in the semantic table and S a set of m components in the student solution on the same level k of the structural hierarchy. $h_k(G, S)$ is a hypothesis of the components on the level k if:*

$h_k(G, S) = \{map(g_i, s_j) | g_i \in G, 1 \leq i \leq n, s_j \in S, 1 \leq j \leq m\}$
and $map(g_p, s_p), map(g_q, s_q) \in h_k \rightarrow g_p \neq g_q, s_p \neq s_q$.

A complete space of hypotheses on the level k is: $H_k := \{h_k(G, S) | h_k(G, S)$ is a hypothesis of the components on the level $k\}$.

The number of hypotheses generated in the sense of Definition 3.8.1 by mapping n elements of the student solution to m elements of the semantic table is calculated according to the following formula:

(1): $|H| = \begin{cases} n!, & \text{if n=m,} \\ \frac{n!}{(n-m)!}, & \text{if n > m,} \\ \frac{m!}{(m-n)!}, & \text{if m > n} \end{cases}$

For example, at the clause level (level 1) of the structural hierarchy of a predicate, a student solution has two clauses $S = \{SC1, SC2\}$ and in the implementation table, a selected generalised solution description has also two clauses $G = \{C1, C2\}$. The complete space of hypotheses on the clause level includes 2! elements:

$H_{clause}(G,S)=\{\{\text{map}(C1,SC1), \text{map}(C2,SC2)\}, \{\text{map}(C2,SC1), \text{map}(C1,SC2)\}\}$[7].

If there exists the level $k + 1$ in the structural hierarchy of a solution, then each element $map_\lambda \in h_k$ will initiate a new hypothesis generation on the level $k+1$ and results in $H_{k+1}(map_\lambda)$ elements according to Formula (1). For each h_k, the number of hypotheses generated on level $k + 1$ is calculated by multiplying the number of the complete space of hypotheses generated for each element map_λ: $\prod_{x=1}^{|h_k|} |H_{k+1}(map_\lambda)|$. The total number of hypotheses which can be generated on the level $k + 1$ is the sum of all hypotheses generated from each element h_k:

$|H_{k+1}| = \sum_{y=1}^{|H_k|} 1 \prod_{x=1}^{|h_k|} |H_{k+1}(map_\lambda)|$

---

[7]To simplify the presentation, we use the name of the level (e.g., clause level) instead of using the index number (level 1).

3.8. ERROR DIAGNOSIS

For example, the space of hypotheses on the clause level above H_{clause} includes two elements. The first one is {map(C1, SC1), map(C2, SC2)} which initiates generating hypotheses on the subgoal level (level 2). If map(C1, SC1) generates $|H(map_1)|$ elements and map(C2, SC2) generates $|H(map_2)|$ elements according to Formula (1), then the first hypothesis of H_{clause} initiates generating $|H(map_1)| * |H(map_2)|$ new hypotheses on the level 2 of the structural hierarchy. Assuming the second element of H_{clause} initiates generating $|H(map_3)| * |H(map_4)|$ hypotheses. In total, on the second level, $|H(map_1)| * |H(map_2)| + |H(map_3)| * |H(map_4)|$ hypotheses are generated.

A hypothesis about a student's solution variant includes hypotheses on each level of the structural hierarchy: $h(solution) := \bigcup_k^K h$, where K is the number of levels of a structural hierarchy.

Depending on the number of levels and the number of components on each level of the structural hierarchy, the space of hypotheses can become very large. As a consequence, the subsequent hypothesis evaluation process would be resource intensive, and the resulting long response time would not be acceptable for a tutoring system. Therefore, it is necessary to narrow down the space of hypotheses to an acceptable size as long as the accuracy of the error diagnosis is still acceptable. One way is restricting the space of hypotheses by taking *matching rules* into account to build only the meaningful hypotheses. For example, clauses of type base case in the student solution should only be mapped to clauses of the same type in the semantic table.

In addition, Beam search, a heuristic technique normally used to solve constraint satisfaction problems (Bain et al., 2004), can be exploited to restrict the space of generated hypotheses. Beam search uses breadth-first search to build its search tree. At each level of the tree, it generates all successors of the states at the current level, sorts them in order of increasing heuristic values, and stores a pre-determined number (which is called the *Beam criterion*) of states at each level.

While the standard Beam search technique deploys the Beam criterion immediately to restrict the generation of search paths, we need to apply the Beam criterion after the inspection of the alternatives. This is caused by the fact that the plausibility of hypotheses is measured by the accumulated constraint weights and constraints can only be applied to complete mappings. Therefore, the space of hypotheses can only be pruned after the complete space of hypotheses has been generated on each level. Only a number of the most plausible hypotheses are taken. Still by reducing the number of promising hypotheses on a lower level, a smaller set of combinations with hypotheses on a higher level have to be checked. This leads to a reduction of the global space.

CHAPTER 3. A COACHING SYSTEM FOR LOGIC PROGRAMMING

Since the approach takes local decisions to narrow down the space of hypotheses, it does not require as much resources as a complete search. However, it may produce less accurate error diagnoses because we leave out hypotheses which do not lie within the Beam criterion. Which approach of hypothesis generation (restricted or unrestricted hypothesis space) should be used depends on the depth and the width of the structural hierarchy. Empirical results on the generation of hypotheses for implementation are given in Section 3.8.4.

3.8.2 Hypothesis Evaluation

The plausibility of each generated hypothesis H is evaluated based on the relevant constraints. The plausibility score is computed multiplying the scores of all constraint violations according to the following formula:

(2): $Plausibility(H) = \prod_{i=1}^{N} W_i$, where W_i is the weight of a violated constraint.

That score is used to decide on the most plausible hypothesis about the student's solution variant. A higher plausibility score corresponds to a more plausible hypothesis. Based on the selection of the best hypothesis, diagnostic information about shortcomings of the student solution can be derived from the constraint violations.

We apply the general process of error diagnosis described above to diagnose errors in the predicate signature and the implementation. The specific procedures are referred to as *signature diagnosis* and *implementation diagnosis*, respectively.

3.8.3 Signature Diagnosis

Hypothesis Generation

In order to generate hypotheses about the student's predicate signature, it is matched against the corresponding components specified in the signature table. The component types of a predicate signature are predicate name, argument positions, an argument's meaning, data type and calling mode. The structural hierarchy of a predicate signature includes two levels (cf. Figure 3.3).

On the first level, the predicate name and the argument positions of the student's predicate signature are matched to components of the same type in the signature table. The size of the complete space of hypotheses generated at this level is computed according to Formula (1), because the student is allowed to specify the argument positions in an arbitrary order. Since the number of argument positions required for a predicate is usually low, and the structural hierarchy of a predicate signature has few levels, it is possible to generate the complete space of hypotheses about a student's predicate signature. Once the hypotheses on the first level have been generated, the matching process continues on the second level to map the components

3.8. ERROR DIAGNOSIS

of an argument position (argument's meaning, data type and calling mode) of the student's predicate signature to the corresponding entries in the signature table. This matching results in one bijective mapping because an argument position consists of only one component of type meaning, one of data type and one of calling mode. Also the matching rules, which allow the matching process to only map components of the same type, are taken into account. For example, consider the following signature for the problem *Investment* provided by the student.

Predicate name invest

Argument	Type	Calling Mode	Meanings
Arg1	Number	Input	"Money"
Arg2	Number	Input	"Rate"
Arg3	Number	Input	"Period"
Arg4	List	Input	"Return"

The student has specified four argument positions. The signature table (Table 3.2) has also been specified with four argument positions for this problem. Hence, the signature diagnosis process generates $4! = 24$ signature mappings. One of them is the following hypothesis mapping Y which consists of 4 entries representing the mapping of four pairs of argument positions. Each entry has two parts. The left part represents information about each argument position specified in the signature table, whereas the right one corresponds to the specification provided by the student. Each part consists of a predicate name, an identifier for each argument position, a calling mode, a data type, and an appropriate meaning concept identified in the problem description.

Hypothesis Y=
{map((p, Arg4, output, number, *Return*), (invest, Arg4, input, list, *Return*)),
map((p, Arg3, input, number, *Period*), (invest, Arg3, input, number, *Period*)),
map((p, Arg2, input, number, *Rate*), (invest, Arg2, input, number, *Rate*)),
map((p, Arg1, input, number, *Money*), (invest, Arg1, input, number, *Money*))}

Hypothesis Evaluation

After the hypotheses have been generated, the plausibility of each hypothesis is computed by checking declaration constraints. The most plausible hypothesis is the mapping which yields the highest plausibility score. Based on the best hypothesis, we are able to infer the signature of the predicate which the student intends to implement.

In the example above, after computing the plausibility of 24 signature mappings, the mapping Y is considered the most plausible one, because it has the highest plausibility score. It violates two declaration constraints.

The first one examines the calling mode of each argument position. It is violated by the input mode of the 4th argument position which represents a return on investment because this should be specified with an output calling mode.

The second constraint examines the data type of argument positions. It is violated by the list data structure specified for the 4th argument position because a return on investment should be a number, not a list. Derived from the two constraint violations, the following hints are returned to the student to help her working on the task analysis.

Hint 1 The calling mode for the 4th argument position is not appropriate. Input mode is used to represent any information given in the problem statement. Do you really want to use "Return" as input? Consult the problem statement again.

Hint 2 The type of the 4th argument position is not appropriate. Do you really want to use "'Return" as a list? Consult the problem statement again.

3.8.4 Implementation Diagnosis

Hypothesis Generation and Evaluation

Once the system has accepted the predicate signature provided by the student, i.e., no declaration constraint is violated, she is allowed to implement the intended predicate. Given a predicate implementation, the error diagnosis process generates hypotheses about it by matching the student implementation against each of the generalised solution descriptions. The matching process results in the space of hypotheses $H_{strategy} = \{\text{map}(gsd_1, \text{SP}), \text{map}(gsd_2, \text{SP}),...\}$, where SP is the student implementation, gsd_i is a generalised solution description specified in the implementation table, and $\text{map}(gsd_i, \text{SP})$ represents a *global mapping*. This level of matching is referred to as *strategy level*. Global mappings are used to find an answer for the question (cf. Section 1.3): Which solution strategy did the student choose?

Then, it is required to generate hypotheses about the student's implementation variant on each level of the structural hierarchy. Since a predicate forms a structural hierarchy of five levels (cf. Figure 3.1), the matching process on the strategy level initiates matching on each level of the structural hierarchy. The matching process maps the components of the student implementation against the corresponding ones of the selected generalised solution level after level. The matching process results in *local mappings* which represent hypotheses about the student's implementation variant on each level of the structural hierarchy. They are used to build global mappings and to find an answer for the question (cf. Section 1.3): How did the student implement the chosen solution strategy?

3.8. ERROR DIAGNOSIS

Once the hypotheses on the strategy level have been generated, i.e., the global mappings are completely filled with local mappings, the second step of the implementation diagnosis process is evaluating each hypothesis with respect to its plausibility using implementation constraints. The hypothesis on the strategy level which has the highest plausibility score is considered the most plausible one. The generalised solution description which has been chosen for that hypothesis is taken as the solution strategy being implemented in the student program. Diagnostic information is derived from constraint violations resulting from the plausibility computation of the selected hypothesis.

In principle, the space of hypotheses about the student's implementation variant on each level of the structural hierarchy could be generated completely. However, this would result in a very large space, because the structural hierarchy of an implementation has many levels and on the subgoal level many subgoals may exist. Therefore, we deploy a Beam criterion to restrict the space of hypotheses.

The plausibility of each generated hypothesis can be used as a Beam criterion to restrict the space of hypotheses to the most plausible ones: Only a fraction of z ($0 \leq z \leq 1$) most plausible hypotheses of the complete space are selected for each level. If $z=1$, the restricted space of hypotheses becomes maximal. The special case $z=0$ means that the restricted space includes only one best hypothesis for each level. In order to choose the best value z for hypothesis generation, we vary the value z and notice the time consumption of the error diagnosis for a number of student implementations. We have run INCOM on 52 student implementations of six different problems including the problem *Investment*. Table 3.6 shows the relation between time consumption and diagnostic accuracy which is determined using a gold standard (which is described in Section 5.2). The first column represents the Beam value. The second column shows how much time the system needed for diagnosis per problem and the third column indicates whether the diagnosis is accurate. The error diagnosis is considered accurate, if each of diagnosed errors are in accordance with the specified gold standard. The table points out that for z below 0.3, the error diagnosis becomes inaccurate. The standard guideline for ideal web response times (Nielsen, 1993) suggests that a response time above 10 seconds can be considered unacceptable, the user is likely to leave the site or system. Hence, the time consumed by INCOM to diagnose a student solution is acceptable, because even for the highest Beam criterion z the error diagnosis maximally consumes 3.2522 seconds.

Algorithms

The process of implementation diagnosis includes two loops of hypothesis ge-neration and hypothesis evaluation (cf. Algorithm 1). The outer loop is generating and evaluating global

Table 3.6: Time consumption and diagnostic accuracy

Beam	Time (sec)	Is diagnosis accurate?
1.0	3.2522	Yes
0.9	3.2942	Yes
0.8	3.1984	Yes
0.7	1.8806	Yes
0.6	1.7405	Yes
0.5	1.7953	Yes
0.4	1.7345	Yes
0.3	1.7026	No
0.2	1.7037	No
0.1	1.7029	No
0.0	1.5801	No

mappings whereas local mappings (of clauses, head/subgoals, arguments/functors, multiplication terms, factors/algebraic signs) are generated and evaluated in the inner loop. The outer loop starts with matching the student implementation against each of the generalised solution descriptions. This calls the inner loop to generate local mappings on the levels of structural components. After the local mappings on the deepest level (arguments/functors if no arithmetic expression exists, or factors/algebraic signs if arithmetic expressions exist) have been generated, their plausibility is evaluated, and the best ones are selected using the Beam criterion. The best selected local mappings on the lower level are used to multiply the space of local mappings on the next higher level. This procedure of generating hypotheses, selecting the best ones using the Beam criterion, and multiplying the space of local mappings of the next level continues up to the clause level, the highest one of the structural hierarchy. At this level, the process of generating global mappings is completed. The outer loop is finished by evaluating the global mappings with respect to their plausibility and choosing the best global mapping for the selected generalised solution description.

If arithmetic expressions are to be matched, the expressions of the student solution and the ones in the semantic table are decomposed according to the rules defined in Section 3.1.1. Matching an arithmetic expression of a student implementation against a corresponding one specified in the implementation table means matching the multiplication terms and factors/algebraic signs. The space of variants of arithmetic expressions can be extended by transforming the arithmetic expressions in the semantic table using the transformation rules described in Section 3.7.3. In case, the student uses neutral arithmetic expressions, e.g., X is $A - 1 + 1$, the system will indicate that the neutral expression $-1 + 1$ is superfluous. Such a system's feedback is justified, because this superfluous term is not useful. Algorithm 2 implements this

3.8. ERROR DIAGNOSIS

Input: GSD: A set of generalised solution descriptions; SP: a student implementation; z: the Beam criterion
Output: A set of best global mappings for each of the generalised solution descriptions

foreach $gsd \in GSD$ **do**
    Generate mappings of clauses between gsd and SP;
    foreach *clause mapping HC* **do**
        Generate mappings of subgoals;
        foreach *subgoal mapping HG* **do**
            if *subgoal is a arithmetic calculation* **then**
                Generate mappings of arithmetic expressions (see Algorithm 2) Select the best arithmetic expression mappings using Beam criterion z;
            end
            else
                Generate mappings of arguments;
                foreach *argument mapping HA* **do**
                      Evaluate the plausibility of each argument mapping HA;
                end
                Select the best argument mappings using Beam criterion z;
            end
            Evaluate the plausibility of each subgoal mapping HG;
        end
        Select the best subgoal mappings using Beam criterion z;
        Evaluate the plausibility of each clause mapping HC;
    end
    Choose the best clause mapping for the selected gsd;
end

Algorithm 1: The algorithm of generating hypotheses about the strategy implemented in a solution

generation of mappings for arithmetic expressions.

> **Input**: SUT: a set of summands of an arithmetic expression specified the semantic table; SU: A set of summands specified in the student implementation; z: the Beam criterion
> **Output**: The most plausible mapping of arithmetic expressions
> Generate mappings of summands between SUT and SU;
> **foreach** *summand mapping SM* **do**
> > Generate mappings of factors/algebraic signs;
> > **foreach** *factor/algebraic sign mapping FM* **do**
> > > Evaluate plausibility of FM;
> >
> > **end**
> > Select the best factor/sign mappings using Beam criterion z;
> > Evaluate plausibility of each summand mapping SM;
>
> **end**
> Return arithmetic expression mappings including summand mappings and factor/algebraic sign mappings;

Algorithm 2: The algorithm of matching arithmetic expressions

The inner loop of the implementation diagnosis generates and evaluates local mappings on the levels of components according to Algorithms 3 and 4, respectively.

Figure 3.4 illustrates the flow of the implementation diagnosis. We notice that along the process of implementation diagnosis, implementation constraints are invoked two times: 1) to evaluate local mappings, and 2) to evaluate global mappings. Why do we not exploit constraint violations which resulted from evaluating local mappings to evaluate global constraints to reduce resource consumption? The reason is that evaluating local mappings invokes semantic constraints which check the co-reference between the arguments existing within a structural component, e.g., a subgoal, and other arguments outside of it. However, at the time of evaluating a local mapping, the antecedents which should be co-referred with arguments within a component may not be available, because other local mappings have not yet been evaluated. In this case, such semantic constraints may not be relevant, or might be relevant but refer to the wrong antecedents. Thus, they should only be invoked to evaluate global mappings after all local mappings are completely available. This type of semantic constraints has been noted as *context sensitive constraints* in (Foth, 2007, p. 63). Since we focus more on diagnostic accuracy than resource consumption, the process of implementation diagnosis in INCOM invokes all implementation constraints during the evaluation of both local mappings and global mappings.

An Example

Assuming, the student has specified an appropriate signature as follows:

3.8. ERROR DIAGNOSIS

Input: Level K; X: a set of expressions in the semantic table; Y is a set of expressions in the student implementation;
Output: A set Z of local mappings on the level K

initialize $Z=[]$;
if $x \in X$ *contains transformable expressions* **then**
 | apply mathematical transformations to create variants of x and add them to X;
end
if X *is empty and* Y *is not empty* **then**
 | take $y \in Y$;
 | add $map(NIL, y)$ to Z;
else if Y *is empty and* X *is not empty* **then**
 | take $x \in X$;
 | add $map(x, NIL)$ to Z;
else forall the $x \in X$ *and* $y \in Y$ **do**
 | add $map(x, y)$ to Z;
end

Algorithm 3: The algorithm of generating local mappings.

Input: Level K; Z: A set of hypothesis mappings
Output: Plausibility score of each hypotheses

Select constraints for the current diagnosis level;
Compute the plausibility $Plausibility(z)$ for each mapping $z \in Z$;

Algorithm 4: The algorithm of evaluating the plausibility of hypotheses.

CHAPTER 3. A COACHING SYSTEM FOR LOGIC PROGRAMMING

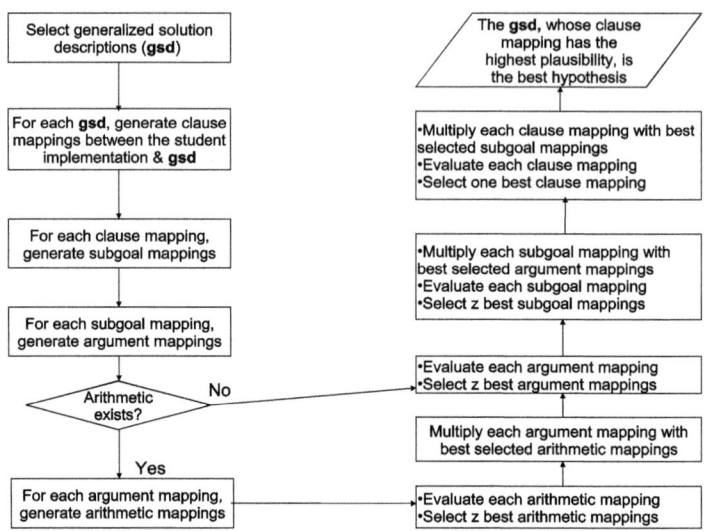

Figure 3.4: The generation of hypotheses about a student implementation

Predicate name	invest			
Argument	**Type**	**Calling Mode**	**Meanings**	
Arg1	Number	Input	"Money"	
Arg2	Number	Input	"Rate"	
Arg3	Number	Input	"Period"	
Arg4	Number	Output	"Return"	

INCOM allows her to implement a predicate to solve the problem *Investment* following any solution strategy she prefers, e.g.:

Clause	**Type**	**Implementation**
SC1	base	invest(S,_, 0, S).
SC2	recursive	invest(S, Z, A, E):- Ab is A-1, invest(S,Z,Ab,E), E is S*(1+Z).

According to the algorithm of the error diagnosis, the student implementation is matched to each of the generalised solution descriptions. First, it is matched to the generalised solution description of the analytic strategy. Then, the matching process successively iterates through the tail recursive, the recursive and arithmetic_after, as well as the recursive and arithmetic_before strategy.

In this example, the matching between the student implementation and the ge-neralised

3.8. ERROR DIAGNOSIS

solution description of the strategy *recursive and arithmetic_before* (cf. Table 3.3) on the clause level results in a single mapping H which has two entries. The first component of each entry represents the expression specified in the generalised solution description and the second one is provided by the student implementation.

H_{clause}={map(C1, SC1), map(C2, SC2)}

Second, on the subgoal level, the subgoals of the student's clause are mapped against the subgoals of the corresponding clause of the generalised solution description. For example, taking the second map of the mapping H above, subgoals of C2 are matched against subgoals of SC2. Considering, for instance, only arithmetic calculation subgoals, matching the two arithmetic calculation subgoals of the student's clause SC2 against two arithmetic calculation subgoals of the generalised solution description's clause C2 results in two mappings of arithmetic subgoals:

$H_{subgoal}$(calculation)={map(NP is P-1, Ab is A-1), map(Ret is NS+R*NS, E is S*(1+Z))}
$H_{subgoal}$(calculation)={map(Ret is NS+R*NS, Ab is A-1), map(NP is P-1, E is S*(1+Z))}

Similarly, the recursive subgoal of the student's clause is mapped to a corresponding subgoal of the recursive clause of the generalised solution description:

$H_{subgoal}$(recursion)={invest(S,Z,Ab,E), inv(S,R,NP,NS)}

In the second clause of the student implementation, there is no arithmetic test for the third argument of the clause head before it is decremented by 1, while in the implementation table (cf. Table 3.3), an arithmetic test for this argument position is required. Thus, it results in the following mapping $H_{subgoal}$(arithmetic test). In total, 2*1*1=2 mappings are generated at this level.

$H_{subgoal}$(arithmetic test)={map(P > 0, NIL)}

Third, on the argument and operator level, the arguments of a student's subgoal are matched against the arguments of the corresponding subgoal of the generalised solution description. For example, the arithmetic subgoal of the student implementation `Ab is A-1` is matched against the subgoal `NP is P-1` of the generalised solution description. Considering the matching rules for arithmetic calculation, e.g., arguments on the left hand side are matched together, and similarly for the arguments on the right hand side:

$H_{argument}$={map(NP, AB), map(P-1, A-1)}

Fourth, on the summand level, the arguments on the right hand side of the arithmetic calculation subgoals are matched. For example, the map(P-1, A-1) yields the following mappings:

$H1_{multiplication}=\{\text{map}(P, A), \text{map}(-1, -1)\}$

$H2_{multiplication}=\{\text{map}(P, -1), \text{map}(-1, A)\}$

Fifth, on the last level, the factors of the student's multiplication term are matched to the ones of the corresponding multiplication term in the generalised solution description, and similarly for algebraic signs. For example, the map(P,-1) results in the following mapping:

$H_{factor}=\{\text{map}(+,-), \text{map}(P,1)\}$

After local mappings have been generated on the factor/algebraic sign level, their plausibility is evaluated by invoking the constraints of that level. Based on the plausibility score of each local mapping, a set of best mappings is selected according the Beam criterion and used to multiply the space of local mappings on the next higher level, namely the multiplication terms. Again, each of the local mappings on the multiplication term level is evaluated with respect to its plausibility. The process of evaluating local mappings, choosing the best ones, and extending the space of mappings on the higher level continues until the clause level is reached. At this level, a space of global mappings for each generalised solution description is established.

We evaluate the plausibility of these global mappings and determine the one which has the highest score for each generalised solution description. According to the first column of Table 3.7, the hypothesis that the student has implemented the strategy *recursive and arithmetic_before* is most plausible because it has the highest plausibility score (0.035). The second column of the table shows diagnoses resulting from the evaluation of each hypothesis. The evaluation of the plausibility of the most plausible hypothesis yields the following diagnostic information:

Hint 1 The variable in **A-1** should be tested against a number.

Hint 2 A co-reference between the argument **S** in the 3rd subgoal and the argument **E** in the 2nd subgoal is required.

Hint 3 The co-reference between the argument **E** in the clause head and the 4th argument in the 2nd subgoal is not necessary.

We have shown in Section 3.8.3 and 3.8.4 that *using the modelling concepts (weighted constraints, semantic table, and transformation rules), it is possible to develop an algorithm to diagnose errors in a logic program and to hypothesize the strategy underlying a solution correctly.* Therefore, Hypothesis 2 has been confirmed.

3.9 Feedback

To be able to help the student on each coaching stage, useful feedback is required. Feedback can take different forms. Fleming and Levie (1993) suggested five types of feedback:

3.9. FEEDBACK

Table 3.7: Plausibility of hypotheses about the implemented solution strategy

Str (Score)	Weight; Hints
1 (0.000001)	0.01; If you want to implement a non-recursive predicate, at least a non-recursive clause must be defined. 0.01; **invest/4** has more base cases than required. 0.01; **invest/4** has more recursive cases than required.
2 (0.005)	0.1; A calculation for the argument **S** in the 2nd subgoal is required. 0.1; A variable in **A-1** should be tested against a number. 0.5; The co-reference between **S** in the clause head and the 1st argument in the 2nd subgoal is not necessary.
3 (0.035)	0.1; The variable in **A-1** should be tested against a number. 0.5; The co-reference between the argument **E** in the clause head and the 4th argument in the 2nd subgoal is not necessary. 0.7; A co-reference between the argument **S** in the 3rd subgoal and the argument **E** in the 2nd subgoal is required.
4 (0.0036015)	0.1; A calculation for the argument **A** in the clause head is required. 0.3; The result of an arithmetic calculation must be passed to the clause head. Unify **Ab** in the 1st subgoal and the 3rd argument in the clause head. 0.5; The co-reference between **E** in the clause head and the 4th argument in the 2nd subgoal is not necessary. 0.7; The 2nd subgoal must be executed before the 1st one. 0.7; The argument **S** in the 3rd subgoal should be co-referenced with the 4th argument in the 2nd subgoal. 0.7; The algebraic sign of the summand **-1** does not satisfy the problem. 0.7; The argument **A** in the 1st subgoal should be co-referenced with the 3rd argument in the 2nd subgoal.

Str 1: Analytic strategy; Str 2: Tail recursive strategy, Str 3: Recursive and arithmetic_before strategy; Str 4: Recursive and arithmetic_after strategy

Confirmation indicates whether a solution is correct or incorrect; *Corrective* feedback provides information about a possible correct response; *Explanatory* feedback explains why a response is incorrect; *Diagnostic* feedback attempts to identify misconceptions by comparing the student solution with common errors; and *elaborative* feedback provides additional related information. Since the constraint-based approach is able to yield error explanations derived from constraint violations, corrective, explanatory and diagnostic feedback can be supported directly. To generate corrective or elaborative feedback, diagnostic results derived from constraint violations need to be processed further and additional information sources are required (e.g., a course book). In this thesis, we focus on explanatory feedback.

3.9.1 Feedback Messages

It is important on which level of programming knowledge a feedback message should be provided. In accordance with general behaviours of programming learners, novice programmers in logic programming often work on the syntax instead of concentrating on the more abstract level (VanSomeren, 1990; Gegg-Harrison, 1999). This issue can be addressed by making high level programming concepts in logic programming explicit to the students. Studies have shown evidence that by teaching high level programming concepts, students acquire remarkable learning effects (Brna, 1993; Návrat and Rozinajová, 1993; Hietala, 1993; Sollohub, 1991).

Several researchers discussed the strengths and weaknesses of the two types of high level knowledge with respect to teaching logic programming. Brna (1993) taught his students logic programming by introducing Prolog programming techniques and requesting them to solve typical Prolog problems. The author reported that his students practiced the application of techniques with interest. However, they found it difficult to choose the appropriate technique as a first step of writing simple programs.

Another approach to making high level programming knowledge in Prolog explicit to students is applying Prolog schemata. When developing Prolog schemata, Gegg-Harrison (1999) had in mind the initial purpose of helping students to learn recursive programming because Prolog is not a keyword-based language and this characteristic makes programming difficult. He proposed a guiding-based approach to tutoring recursive programming. First, a Prolog schema is introduced to the student, and several sample predicates which are instances of that schema are presented. Then, a problem is posed, and the student is requested to fill in the slots of the introduced schema. Similarly, Bieliková and Návrat (1998) applied a schema-based approach to teach programming in Prolog and LISP. The authors presented a catalogue of schemata to the student, explained every schema, and requested her to apply it. The study reported that schemata influenced the student's programming performance positively. However, some researchers doubt its learning effect due to the following reasons. First, although the student might acquire procedural knowledge about high level concepts by applying schemata, the task of filling-in templates might rather help her to memorise the schemata and to adapt code structures (Bowles and Brna, 1999). The student may not understand why the slots of such templates are necessary to solve a given problem. Furthermore, the schema-based tutoring approach does not require the student to address the principles of how the slots of a schema work together. Therefore, she would not be able to transfer the "skill of filling-in slots" into other problem contexts where another program structure is required. Second, filling in the slots of a schema template just satisfies the existence requirement of several schema components. But,

3.9. FEEDBACK

solving a logic programming problem requires more skills than merely filling-in slots (Vasconcelos, 1995), e.g., unification of arguments, determination of the number of required argument positions, determination of argument and subgoal order. That is why the coaching model of INCOM favours to formulate feedback messages in terms of programming techniques to help students develop the skills of using high level programming concepts in logic programming. In addition to the purpose of conveying high level programming concepts to students, feedback messages are also intended to capture basic concepts.

3.9.2 Ranking and Grouping Feedback Messages

By means of constraint weights, feedback derived from constraint violations can be presented in a preferred order, e.g., severe errors are presented first (cf. Table 3.7). In addition, error information of the same hypothesis level can be grouped to establish a contextual connection between different feedback messages. For example, errors on the highest level (clause level) are presented first. In this manner, the student learns to start the implementation with a coarse design first, and then refine it. Thus, Hypothesis 3, that *using constraint weights, it is possible to prioritize feedback according to the importance of errors* can be considered true.

Since Prolog patterns can be modelled using weighted constraints (cf. Section 3.7.2), optionally, *strategy-related feedback messages* can be grouped together and presented in a coherent manner to the student (if a pattern has been found in the student implementation). This should keep the student to concentrate on the strategy she is implementing. Therefore, Hypothesis 4, that *it is possible to create a knowledge base of standard solution strategies in logic programming using weighted constraints and to group feedback messages in a coherent manner* can be accepted.

3.9.3 Error Location

A feedback message could confuse the student, if it does not indicate where the error is located in the student solution. This can happen because the structure of a solution may be very complex and may consist of many components of the same type. Therefore, in addition to a feedback message, a corresponding pointer to the error location is desired. If a student's predicate signature is not appropriate, a feedback message indicates the position of the erroneous component in the structure, e.g., argument mode of an argument position X is not correct. If a student implementation is erroneous, a feedback message is associated with one of the following types of error location with increasing degree of detail: clause, subgoal or clause head, and argument.

3.10 Limitations

Using weighted constraints, semantic table and transformation rules, our approach is able to model a fairly large solution space. Nevertheless, it suffers from two limitations. First, we want that the student develops her creativity as much as possible, e.g., by defining helper predicates in addition to a main predicate. However, it is not always possible to transform a predicate definition using a helper predicate into a predicate definition without using one, e.g., if both the main predicate and the helper predicate require recursion as part of the solution strategy, the unfolding/folding transformation techniques are no longer applicable. For such a case, normally a verifiable complex transformation algorithm needs to be devised. Another way which remains is anticipating and specifying possible helper predicates in the semantic table. Unfortunately, the space of possible helper predicates which students can define is open-ended, and anticipating such helper predicates seems to be impossible. This might be a general limitation for a tutoring system for programming.

The second limitation of our approach is that the diagnostic abilities of the system are strictly limited by the completeness of the entries in the implementation table. In case, a student follows an unexpected but correct strategy, the system chooses from the available generalised solution descriptions the one, which is most similar and "forces" diagnosis on it. In order to overcome this problem, it could be possible to deploy a verifiable transformation algorithm which transforms an implementation of a solution strategy to another strategy, e.g., the transformation algorithm developed by Gegg-Harrison (1993), to extend the space of possible implementation variants used by the student. As a result, the solution strategy invented by the student is considered the same one specified in the implementation table according to Definition 3.1.17 (if an verifiable transformation algorithm could be used). Another approach to overcome this limitation would be to specify strategy-independent requirements for a solution, e.g., based on a formal specification of the task and a model of the semantics of the programming language.

Chapter 4

Implementation

The purpose of this dissertation is to explore the capability of the weighted constraint-based approach in diagnosing errors and to evaluate the usefulness of diagnostic information in terms of improving programming skills in logic programming. INCOM, a tutoring system for logic programming has deployed the conceptual design described in the previous section and has been implemented according to the requirements specified in Section 3.2 to serve both purposes. This chapter gives an overview of the current implementation.

4.1 Architecture

The architecture of INCOM consists of three layers (4.1): user interface, back-end, and knowledge base. The *user interface* is used to present the description of a problem, provide the possibility to read the student solution, and show feedback messages. The *back-end* components (a *parser*, a *matcher*, and a *general constraint evaluator*) process the student input and evaluate her solution to a given problem.

The back-end components work as follows. The parser extracts the student input, reads corresponding information from the semantic table, and transforms both into an internal representation called *assertions*. The matcher tries to match the assertions of the student's input against the ones of the semantic table taking matching rules into consideration. After the matching process has generated hypotheses, the constraint evaluator consults the knowledge base (including the semantic tables and the weighted constraints) to evaluate each hypothesis with respect to its plausibility. The diagnostic information of the best hypothesis is then presented to the student via the user interface.

Since INCOM should be a web-based system to satisfy the requirements specified in Section 3.2, its user interface has been implemented using the Java ServerPages technology. The parser, the matcher, the constraint evaluator, as well as the know-ledge base have been implemented

CHAPTER 4. IMPLEMENTATION

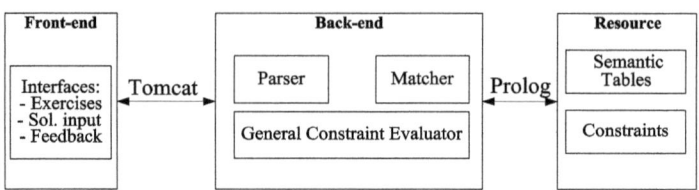

Figure 4.1: The architecture of INCOM

in Prolog. The communication between the user interface and the backend components is established by a Tomcat web-server. Thus, INCOM can be run on every platform where Java, Tomcat and Prolog are available.

4.2 User Interface

The user interface of INCOM has two functionalities which are supported by most programming environments: providing text fields for the solution and displaying diagnostic information. The user interface is divided into three sections (Figure 4.2). The top section is used to display a problem description, the middle one allows the student to input her solution, and feedback messages are displayed iteratively on the bottom section of the interface.

Since INCOM is designed to support the two-stage coaching approach, for each stage it provides an appropriate working environment. Figure 4.2 and Figure 4.3 show the screen layout for the stage of the task analysis and the implementation, respectively.

Corbett et al. (1997) proposed two principles for the design of the problem solving environment of an ITS :

1. The user interface should approximate the real world problem solving environment.

2. The problem solving environment should facilitate the learning process.

The first principle ensures that the student is able to solve similar problems in other environments or in the real world, where the same problem solving environment is not available. The second principle intends to maximize the transfer of domain knowledge to the student. These two principles are conflicting. Using a complex problem solving environment, which reflects the real world, learning is rather hindered because the student needs to understand the functionality of the environment first, before she begins to solve the problems. The student has to consider many interwoven aspects which are not always directly relevant to the problem.

Using the screen layout for the stage of task analysis, the student has to fill in values into pre-specified templates to specify the signature: argument positions, data type, calling

4.3. BACK-END COMPONENTS

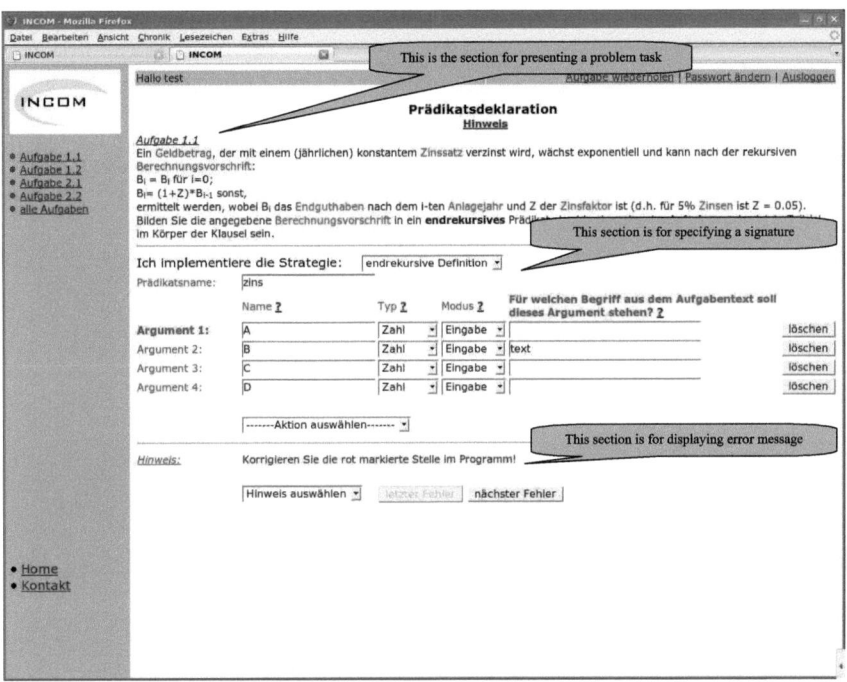

Figure 4.2: The user interface for task analysis.

mode, and meaning. This kind of layout corresponds to the second principle, because from a pedagogical view, it reduces the cognitive load and helps the student to remember what to do when she is requested to specify the predicate signature.

Unlike the working environment for task analysis, where pre-specified structures or menu choices are used, the screen layout for the implementation stage allows the student to input her solution in a free form because the student should be able to develop programming solutions creatively. Although the student is moderately restricted to solution templates (the distinction between a clause head and a clause body is given), this kind of layout still agrees with the first principle above.

4.3 Back-End Components

We assume that the student is able to understand a problem description and system feedback presented by INCOM. In the opposite direction of communication, students' input needs to be

CHAPTER 4. IMPLEMENTATION

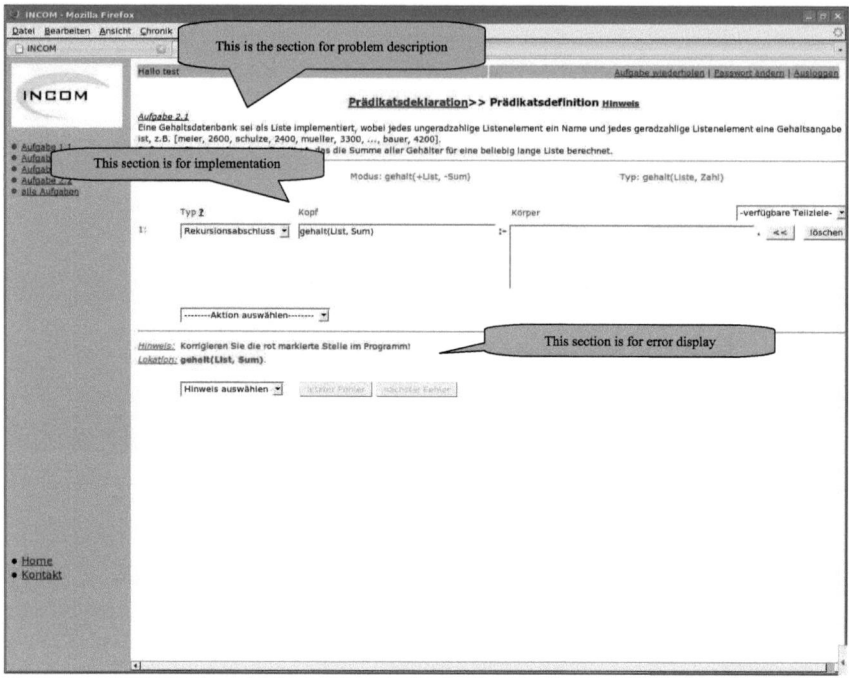

Figure 4.3: The user interface for implementation.

translated into an internal form which can be processed by the system. The *parser* is responsible for this task.

Because the syntax of a Prolog predicate is very simple, the relationship between the components of a predicate implementation needs to be extracted in order to reflect the complete semantics underlying that predicate. Part of the parsing task is supported by the solution templates of the user interface, namely by the slots for each clause (cf. Figure 4.3). The relationships between the components of a predicate are represented by means of the following relational representation:

head_argument(clause index, clause type, helper predicates, head name, head length, argument index, argument type, argument value)

body_argument(clause index, subgoal index, functor, subgoal type, subgoal length, argument index, argument type, argument value)

In addition, the instantiation states of all arguments within a clause also need to be extracted. An instantiation state of an argument is either *instantiated* or *free* and is represented

4.4. KNOWLEDGE BASE

in a relational form:

argument_mode(clause index, subgoal index, argument index, value, instantiation state)

After the assertions *head_argument*, *body_argument*, and *argument_mode* have been extracted from the student solution and the chosen generalised solution description, the *matcher* matches the assertions of the student solution against the ones of the generalised solution description.

The *general constraint evaluator* is implemented using the unification mechanism. After relevant constraints have been selected for evaluation from the knowledge base, the relevance part of each constraint is unified with the available assertions. If the unification is successful, the constraint is relevant and its satisfaction part is unified with the existing assertions. If the second unification is also successful, the constraint is satisfied, otherwise it is violated.

4.4 Knowledge Base

The *knowledge base* consisting of semantic tables and constraints is represented as Prolog relational facts. In order to construct a semantic table for a problem, we collected student solutions from past written examinations and homework assignments. After that, we analysed student solutions aiming at identifying possible solution strategies, which students might have applied. Finally, each identified solution strategy is modelled in the semantic table.

Table 4.1: Number of constraints

Constraint Type	Number
Declaration	15
Implementation	
General principle	7
Pre-implementation	13
Semantic	96
Pattern	16
Total	147

Defining constraints is the knowledge acquisition process which collects principles of the domain and extracts properties of correct solutions for a given problem. We have identified principles of the domain of logic programming from standard works, e.g., (Brna, 2001; Sterling and Shapiro, 1994), and extracted properties of correct solutions based on our corpus of collected student solutions. Currently, the knowledge base of INCOM contains 147 weighted constraints as indicated in Table 4.1 and four patterns (cf. Section 3.1.3).

Chapter 5

Evaluation

5.1 Goals

Systematic evaluations are an essential element of research in the fields which rely on the use of incomplete knowledge components, apply heuristic decision methods, and involve user interactions. In this respect, the tutoring system for logic programming INCOM is concerned with the problem of completeness of its modelling components (weighted constraints, semantic tables, transformation rules), the choice of constraint weights and the usability of the user interface.

The completeness of the model components cannot be checked by local software tests, because the complexity of the system's error diagnosis reaches a high degree even for a relative simple problem. For this reason, a systematic evaluation is necessary for a particular tutoring system. A systematic evaluation can be carried out in different ways and on different levels, e.g., internal vs. external evaluations depending on the development phase the system currently is in.

During the development of a tutoring system, the diagnostic accuracy is most important because it is the foundation, on which a student model is built and feedback is produced. High diagnostic accuracy is one of the requirements of INCOM (cf. Section 3.2). Internal evaluations with respect to diagnostic accuracy are rarely considered when evaluating a tutoring system. Instead, we can find examples of external evaluation methodologies which are based on comparing the learning effectiveness between a control and an experimental group or on the difference between the results of a pre- and a post-test, e.g., (VanLehn et al., 2005; Anderson et al., 1993). One of the reasons for this tendency might be that so far mostly problems have been consi-dered, for which a student has a little room to develop a solution creatively. Thus, for such problems, the evaluation of diagnostic accuracy is not an issue. This situation is different when the student is invited to produce a solution within a large space of possibilities (e.g., alternative solution strategies are possible). Here we need to distinguish the two aspects of diagnosis: 1) Whether the system was able to correctly determine the solution strategy chosen by the student and to identify its components (intention analysis) and 2) whether it was able to correctly diagnose the errors in the student solution (diagnostic validity). For this reason, a study has been conducted in 2008 to evaluate the diagnostic ability of INCOM.

In addition, the end goal of INCOM is to improve students' skills in logic programming, and thus an external evaluation is required to determine to what extent diagnostic information can be used as feedback by the students and whether the two-stage coaching model is useful (cf. the first requirement specification of INCOM in Section 3.2).

5.2 Diagnostic Accuracy

Since the goals of the evaluation of diagnostic accuracy are two-fold, the study is comprised of two parts: evaluating the accuracy of intention analysis and the diagnostic validity. To conduct these experiments, we collected exercises which meet the requirements of INCOM specified in Section 3.2, and solutions from past written examinations. The examination candidates had attended a course in logic programming which was offered as a part of the first semester curriculum in Informatics. The following seven problems have been collected from the written examinations of the years 1999 and 2000. The description for the second problem can be found in Appendix A.

1. Access to specific elements within an embedded list;
2. Querying a data base and applying a linear transformation to the result;
3. Modification of all elements of a list subject to a case distinction;
4. Creation of an n-best list from a data base;
5. Computing the sum of all integer elements of a list;
6. Counting the number of elements in an embedded list;
7. Finding the element of an embedded list which has the maximum value for a certain component.

For these problems, 221 student solutions were selected according to the following criteria:

- Any piece of code which satisfies minimal requirements of interpreting it as a Prolog program is considered a solution,
- syntax errors in the solutions are ignored (because during the written examination the students did not have access to a computer), and

5.2. DIAGNOSTIC ACCURACY

Table 5.1: Evaluation of the intention analysis

Task	Solution	Not Understandable	Correctly A.	Incorrectly A.
1	10	0	10	0
2	11	0	10	1
3	6	2	3	1
4	17	1	16	0
5	58	2	54	2
6	81	0	79	2
7	38	2	34	2
Sum	221	7	206	8

A.: analysed

- both correct and incorrect solutions are taken into account.

After collecting student solutions, each of them was complemented with an appropriate predicate signature, because during the examination, students were not asked to provide that information. Therefore, this evaluation study addressed only the capability of diagnosing errors in student implementations.

5.2.1 Intention Analysis

Design

The evaluation of intention analysis is meant to determine the number of student solutions, which can be analysed and whose solution strategy is identified correctly by the system. In the literature, this kind of evaluation is also noted as *algorithm analysis* (Johnson, 1990; Looi, 1991) because the approach of identifying the solution strategy is based on anticipated algorithms for a programming problem.

The evaluation of intention analysis of INCOM required to involve a human expert who inspected every student solution manually. Student solutions which could not even be understood by the human expert, were sorted out to the group *"not understandable"* (see an example in Appendix G). All *"understandable"* solutions were input into the system which resulted in a list of violated constraints. The human expert examined the list of violated constraints and decided whether the system analysed the student solution correctly. Accordingly, it is assigned to the categories *"correctly analysed"* or *"incorrectly analysed"*.

Results

Table 5.1 summarizes the statistics of the evaluation. The amount of available student solutions is indicated in the second column. The third column represents the number of solutions which are sorted to the category *"not understandable"*. The fourth and the last column show the amount of solutions which belong to the category "*correctly analysed*" and "*incorrectly analysed*", respectively.

On average, 87.9% (s.d.=17.1%) of the collected student solutions could be ana-lysed correctly by INCOM (Le and Menzel, 2008a). The ratio between "*not understandable*" and "*incorrectly analysed*" solutions is 7:8 indicating that almost half of the solutions, for which INCOM is not able to produce a correct analysis, cannot be understood by the human expert either. Those solutions, which could not be understood by the human expert, have been implemented with many arbitrary helper predicates (Appendix G, Example 2).

Two reasons made the analysis of INCOM fail. First, the students tried to define helper predicates which were not included in the semantic table. This is a limitation of the semantic table which has been used to model the space of implementations (cf. Section 3.10). Second, the system's parser interpreted the solutions differently from the intention of the student. For instance, the expression `G2 is G*1,02` can be understood by a German human expert because in German the decimal comma is used instead of a decimal point, but was misinterpreted by the system as a concatenation of two subgoals: `G2 is G1 and 02`.

5.2.2 Diagnostic Validity

Design

The goal of evaluating the diagnostic validity is to determine whether the diagnostic result is acceptable with respect to a gold standard which is specified by human experts of a domain. The task of specifying a gold standard is not easy because by adopting individual perspectives or preferences, human experts tend to disagree in their judgements as the complexity of problems is increasing. If agreement can be established at all, still resource requirements are high. Therefore, any gold standard in an open-ended domain is a compromise between the desirable and the possible.

In other systems, e.g., PROUST, APROPOS2 and Hong's Prolog tutor, the gold standard for evaluating the diagnostic ability has been specified by hand analysis. That is, a human expert analysed each student solution and detected errors independent from any diagnostic result. The list of detected errors is used as a gold standard against which the diagnostic validity of the system is checked. However, it is difficult to specify such a gold standard for a constraint-based system because of the following reasons. First, the human expert has to know the large set of constraints (at the time of this evaluation study, INCOM included about 110 constraints) which represent error types, and relate every error detected in a program to a corresponding constraint. This is a very laborious undertaking for a human expert. Second, a constraint can be relevant to a solution many times. If a human expert has to assign a

5.2. DIAGNOSTIC ACCURACY

Table 5.2: Categories for Precision and Recall

	Should-be errors	Should-not errors
Retrieved errors	A	B
Not retrieved errors	C	

detected error to one of the existing constraints, she would have to iterate through the list of constraints as many times as the system does. This is a bothersome and error prone task. Hence, we specified the gold standard in a way that provides a balance between human and system orientation.

A human tutor of the logic programming course has been invited to check all errors diagnosed by INCOM for every student solution, either confirming or rejecting it. In addition, the human tutor had the possibility to give a comment to each of the errors. Finally, he had the option to add general comments which are not specific to the presented errors, for example, if he thought that crucial errors have been missed. The gold standard is derived from both the system's diagnosis and the comments of the human expert. For the evaluation, we only selected student solutions which have been classified as *understandable* by a human tutor, a category which has already been used for the evaluation of the intention analysis.

Results

To measure diagnostic validity, well known measures from information retrieval (Rijsbergen, 1979) are applied, since both are subset selection problems sharing the same kind of error characteristics: over-generation (too many bugs have been reported) or under-generation (too few bugs have been reported). In such a situation, Recall and Precision are appropriate quality measures, which are defined with respect to Table 5.2 as follows:

$$Recall = \frac{A}{A+C} \quad ; \quad Precision = \frac{A}{A+B}$$

The categories *retrieved* and *not-retrieved* errors are produced by the system's diagnosis, whereas *should-be* and *should-not* errors need to be determined by human judges. Under these definitions a high precision means that the model is based on fairly reliable constraints, which have a low risk of producing false alarms, i.e., the developer was careful to avoid particularly risky constraints. A high recall, on the other hand, means that the diagnosis has a good coverage, i.e., it considers a sufficiently rich set of relevant constraints.

Table 5.3 summarizes the results of system diagnoses of INCOM (Le and Menzel, 2008b). It shows that with values between 0.901 and 1.000 recall is high. That means, the constraint set of the system has been well developed and the knowledge base of the domain is large enough. We also notice that precision is always lower than recall. That is, the diagnosis emphasises quantity more than quality. In particular, the low precision of Task 1 points to a particular

Table 5.3: Evaluation of the diagnostic validity

Task	1	2	3	4	5	6	7	Average
Recall	0.948	1.000	1.000	0.901	1.000	0.981	0.952	0.969
Precision	0.843	0.875	1.000	0.891	0.974	0.953	0.952	0.927

weakness of the constraints relevant for this problem task.

Two main classes of errors which have been marked as false diagnosis by the human tutor can be identified. The first one relates to cases where the constraints are too rigid. For instance, at the time of this evaluation, INCOM did not allow a constant to be assigned to a variable using the operator **is**, e.g., *X is 0*, although 0 is a valid arithmetic expression. Therefore, the human tutor considered this kind of error detected by INCOM not acceptable. The second class of errors which have been interpreted as false diagnosis by the human tutor occurred when two arguments of a subgoal are swapped. In this case, the system detected several errors: e.g., superfluous/missing co-reference between two variables (cf. Section 3.8.4). Instead of receiving many errors considering co-references between variables, the human tutor expected a more compact feedback which should show the student what she has to do. To remove this deficiency of INCOM, diagnostic results need to be compressed similar to the proposal in (Menzel, 1992).

There were seven student solutions which have been implemented using helper predicates, but could not be understood correctly by the system. The system INCOM has been extended with the ability to correctly process them. In the most recent evaluation, the performance of the intention analysis of INCOM raised to 90.8%.

5.2.3 Related Work and Discussion

To check whether the diagnostic ability of INCOM is competitive, we compare it with results from PROUST (Johnson, 1990), APROPOS2 (Looi, 1991), and Hong's Prolog tutor (Hong, 2004) with respect to the intention analysis and diagnostic validity because these systems provide similar difficult problems, e.g., the rainfall problem (PROUST), the list reversal problem (APROPOS2 and Hong's Prolog tutor), which can be assigned to the third class of the problem classification (cf. Section 2.4). In PROUST, programming plans are used to perform intention-based diagnosis of errors in PASCAL programs, APROPOS2 follows an algorithm-based approach, and Hong's Prolog tutor applies a transformation technique to diagnose errors in Prolog programs. These systems have been evaluated based on the following measures: 1) the percentage of programs whose solution strategy is identified correctly, 2) the percentage of correctly recognised (not recognised) errors, and 3) number of false alarms which are errors

5.2. DIAGNOSTIC ACCURACY

detected by the systems but not noted by a human tutor. Note, that for these systems no learning benefits have been reported yet. We compare INCOM with these three systems by calculating the Recall and Precision measures based on the statistics reported in the corresponding literature and under the assumption that the gold standard of these systems has been specified comparably.

The comparison in Table 5.4 shows that PROUST is superior with respect to intention analysis (96%)[1] but its precision (0.88) is lowest. Hong's Prolog tutor achieves the highest precision (1.0), however, at the cost of a low recall (0.69). Overall, INCOM combines an acceptable quality of intention analysis (90.8%) with a high diagnostic accuracy (0.93) compared to the other systems. Note, the method we used to determine the gold standard is based on actual system diagnoses. Therefore, it seems that the precision of the system's diagnosis is too optimistic.

Table 5.4: A comparison of the diagnostic accuracy

System	Intention Analysis	Precision	Recall
INCOM	90.8%	0.9266	0.9688
PROUST	96%	0.8787	0.8143
APROPOS2	80%	0.9580	0.9913
Hong's Prolog tutor	80%	1.0000	0.6886

With respect to evaluating the diagnostic validity, our methodology shares a fundamental shortcoming with other methods because it assumes that "the correctness of diagnoses can be unambiguously determined" (Legree et al., 1993). Unfortunately, this assumption is not realistic in a domain like logic programming which allows alternative solution strategies and different implementation variants. Therefore, a second human expert, namely the system developer, was asked to assess the comments provided by the first human expert, and conflicting opinions were expected. Indeed, while defining the gold standard for our evaluation of diagnostic validity, the system developer did not agree with 3 of 535 comments which the human expert made for the system's diagnosis while specifying the gold standard. The disagreement was eventually resolved by directly negotiating the gold standard.

The use of recall and precision helps us to tailor the diagnosis according to our requirements. In our opinion, a coaching system would be more useful if it could provide an extensive knowledge base. That is, recall should be maximized. However, if recall increases, precision might decrease because the diagnosis could become less accurate if a wider range of bugs is

---

[1] Note, in this evaluation both complete and partial analyses have been counted as positive, and we take only the statistics of the problem Rainfall into account.

considered. The recall value of our system is higher than the precision. This agrees with our intention.

5.3 Learning Effect

The evaluation of learning effect aims at answering the question whether students improve their programming skills after using the system INCOM. The study was conducted with students who were attending a course in logic programming. The experiment took place in the computer pools of the Department of Informatics, University of Hamburg during regular classroom hours, where normally students are expected to demonstrate their homework in the presence of a human tutor. The students were given credits for participating in the study but had the possibility to opt out. The students were separated into two groups: a control and an experimental group. In order to balance the two groups in terms of students' performance and size, the achievement score of the preceding sessions for each student was summed up, and the two groups were balanced using these scores so that the difference between the total scores of the two groups was minimal. Students, who came late, were allowed to join the experiment, but were not taken as valid cases of the study. This study includes two evaluation sessions (in order to enrich the evaluation data): the first one took place in 2009 and the second one in January 2010. In the first session, three invalid cases were not considered and in the second one, four invalid cases were removed. Table 5.5 shows the size of the control group and the experimental one after omitting invalid cases. We assume that the participants of two experiment sessions were not the same students[2].

Table 5.5: Number of experiment participants

Round	Control Group	Experimental Group
1	17	18
2	16	16

5.3.1 Design

A pre-test was administered to both control and experimental group in order to ensure initial comparability on the dependent measures. The students were required to complete the pre-test within 10 minutes. After that, they were given five problems (Appendix C) which were collected from the homework and examinations of former years of the same course. The time for this part of experiment session was limited to 60 minutes. The participants of the experimental group were asked to read a short tutorial (Appendix B) which explains the user interface of

---

[2]If a student cannot pass the examination, she is allowed to attend the course again.

5.3. LEARNING EFFECT

the system. The participants of the control group were provided with the normal environment consisting of an editor and an interpreter (in our case SWI-Prolog). Both the system INCOM and the Prolog interpreter were started before the experiment session begun.

A post-test (to be completed within 10 minutes) was given to the participants of both groups after completion of the experiment session. Pre- and post-test were made comparable by a counter-balanced design of the test items. Specifically, two test versions were developed: Test A (Appendix A) and Test B (Appendix D). Test A was assigned as pre-test and Test B as post-test to 50% of the participants of the control group, and the rest of the control group had Test B as pre-test and Test A as post-test. The same was done for the experimental group.

At the end, the students of the experimental group were given a questionnaire (Appendix E) in order to express their opinions about the usefulness of the system. The participants of the other group were given questions about the difficulty of the test and experiment exercises. Student solutions of tests and of experiment exercises were collected to be used for analysis. In addition, students' responses to the questionnaire were used as subjective data. The whole process including pre-test, experiment session, post-test, and questionnaire was limited to 90 minutes.

5.3.2 Results

Learning Gains

A pre or post-test could be scored maximally with nine points. Comparing the results of the pre-test of the control and the experimental group, we did not find a statistically significant difference ($p=0.07$ for the first session and $p=0.48$ for the second one with a significance level of 0.05). Therefore, we can assume that the groups were fairly balanced.

In order to determine whether the system is effective in improving the programming skills of the students, learning gains were calculated as the difference between post-test and pre-test scores. Table 5.6 shows the development of scores from pre-test to post-test. The third column represents the learning gains of each group and of each experiment session. The last column shows whether the difference between pre- and post-test is statistically significant (at the 5% level). The table shows that during the first session the experimental group made a significant improvement (Gain=1.25; $p<0.01$) whereas the control group did not (Gain=0.74; $p=0.27$). During the second session, both groups did achieve significant learning gains.

Difference Between The Experimental Group and The Control Group

The indicator of learning gains clearly shows that the participants of the experimental group of both evaluation sessions improved their programming skills. However, the control

Table 5.6: Learning gains

Group	Session	Learning gains (s.d.)	Significant (p value)
Control	1	0.74 (2.64)	No (0.27)
Experimental	1	1.25 (1.81)	Yes (0.01)
Control	2	1.28 (1.45)	Yes (0.003)
Experimental	2	1.81 (1.79)	Yes (0.001)

group made progress on average as well (though this was not statistically significant for the control group of the first session).

In order to compare the improvement between the experimental and the control group, we compute the effect size Cohen's d[3] as a standardized mean difference between the two groups.

Table 5.7 summarizes the learning gains of the two experiment sessions. The third column of the table shows that in both sessions the learning gains of the experimental group were not significantly better than the one of the control group. At the first session the effect size of learning gains between the experimental and the control group is small (d=0.23). According to (Wolf, 1986), this effect size indicates an educational significance, i.e., something was learned due to the use of INCOM compared to a standard programming environment. The learning effect of the second session was better than at the previous one (d=0.33), although it is also small. In general, in both sessions, the results show a stable trend of the development of learning gains of the experimental group: the experimental group did outperform the control group by a small effect size between 0.23 and 0.33 standard deviations.

Table 5.7: The effect size Cohen's d

Session	LG(Con)>LG(Exp)	Cohen's d
1	p=0.50	0.23
2	p=0.36	0.33

Students Attitude

Based on a questionnaire, we identified the attitude of participants towards the system. It contained the following questions, for each question, participants were asked to provide their opinion on a scale between 1 (very negative) and 5 (very positive). We accumulated the results of the questionnaire of two experiment sessions.

1. Is the user interface comprehensible?
2. Did the two-stage coaching model help you?

[3]$d = \frac{gain(experimental) - gain(control)}{\sqrt{\frac{variance(experimental) + variance(control)}{2}}}$; Cohens Rules-of-Thumb: small effect (d=0.2), medium effect (d=0.5), large effect (d>0.8)

5.3. LEARNING EFFECT

3. How precise is the information about the location of the error?
4. How comprehensible are the system hints?
5. Did system hints motivate you to continue working on your solutions?
6. Did the system help you to find a solution for a problem task?
7. Would you be able to solve other problems of the same type as the experiment exercises?
8. Would you use this system to do your homework?
9. How difficult did you find the exercises?[4]

With respect to the difficulty of the experiment exercises, 50% of the participants (of the control and the experimental group) rated from difficult to very difficult and 21% of them found the exercises simple or very simple.

Figure 5.1 shows that most students agreed that the system was able to provide precise error location (44%) and the proportion of participants who rated feedback messages positively is as high as the one who rated negatively (39%). However, with respect to the user interface and the two-stage coaching strategy, a high number of participants were not satisfied (Figure 5.2).

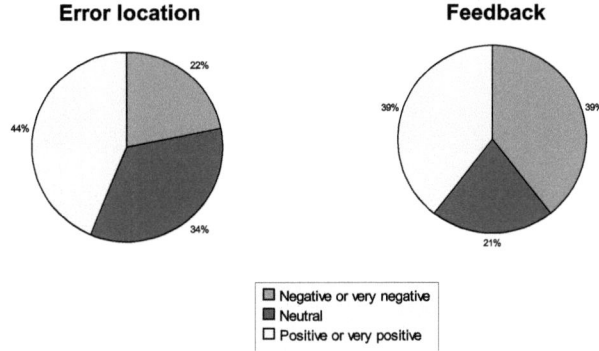

Figure 5.1: Participants' ratings on the precision of error location and the expressiveness of feedback messages

Overall, the participants were motivated to work with the system (56%) and they felt confident to solve problems of the same type (46%) (Figure 5.3). However, a relative high proportion of participants (47%) denied the helpfulness of the system and 59% of them would not deploy the system for homework (Figure 5.4). Despite this cautious self-assessment, the

---
[4] For this question, an answer with 1 indicates "very difficult", and 5 for "very simple".

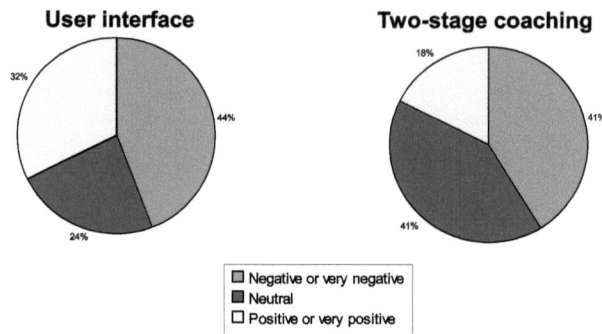

Figure 5.2: Participants' ratings on the user interface and the tutoring model

statistic results in the previous section showed that at least some of them have made moderate learning gains.

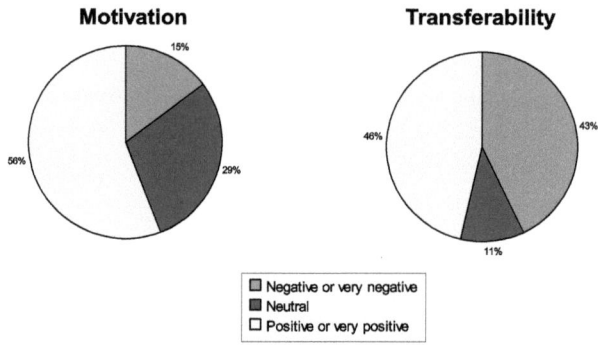

Figure 5.3: Participants' ratings on their motivation and their transferability

In addition to the nine questions in the questionnaire, the participants of the experimental group had the opportunity to express their opinion about the system INCOM freely. Thirteen of total 34 participants gave free comments which are summarized in Table 5.8. Unfortunately, all the comments refer to negative aspects of the system.

5.3.3 Related Work and Discussion

In this evaluation study, both the empirical data (pre/post-test statistics) and the subjective students' attitudes towards the system gave evidence that the system has helped students to improve their skills in logic programming. The empirical results indicated that the students who

5.3. LEARNING EFFECT

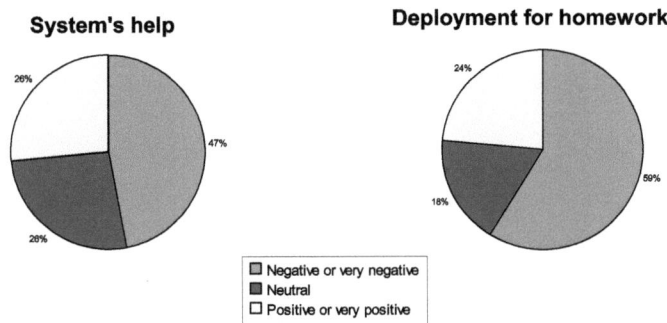

Figure 5.4: Participants' ratings on the helpfulness and the deployment of the system

Table 5.8: Free comments provided by the experimental group

Comment	Participant #
System requires much more time to become familiar with	6
Feedback is helpful, but does not point to a corrective action	2
System is useful, but restrictive	3
System is slow	2

used the system outperformed the control group by between 0.23 and 0.33 standard deviation. Given the degree of difficulty of the problems to be solved and the relatively short exposure time of 60 minutes, this is a remarkable result. Other studies with different systems and within different tutoring domains reported higher learning gains but after longer tutoring periods as shown in Table 5.9. However, a truly long-term study makes extremely difficult to factor out properly the various contributions which might have influenced the learning process.

Table 5.9: Learning benefits of different tutoring systems for programming

System	Period	Effect size
INCOM	60 minutes	0.23-0.33 s.d.
LISP tutor	1 semester	1.00 s.d.
SQL tutor	120 minutes	0.65 s.d.

In addition to the statistical results, the responses to a questionnaire confirmed the usefulness of diagnostic information provided by INCOM: students were motivated to continue working on their individual solution. *Therefore, we can conclude that Hypothesis 5 (cf. Section 1.5) is true.*

Similar to a classroom session where a human tutor would expect that students achieve learning gains within 90 minutes, the study has also demonstrated that students who used

INCOM for the same period did improve their programming skills. The study, however, was not able to identify the most relevant factors contributing to this improvement. It could be accounted to the feedback of the system, to the guidance of the user interface which forces students to work systematically, or even to the recall of previously learned concepts by being exposed to the terminology of the user interface and the system feedback.

We take the subjective results seriously and attempt to find out which reasons lead to the attitude that most students denied the helpfulness and the deployment of the system for homework. There may be several reasons. First, the students may be not aware about their learning progress while using the system because the time of using the system was too short.

Second, they needed much time to become familiar with the functionality of the system. Five of total thirteen comments addressed this issue. Note, not all of the participants did give comments. In particular, participants of the experimental group spent between 29% (at the second session) and 36% (at the first session) of 60 minutes to analyse the five programming tasks. This is a remarkable amount of time compared to the remaining time for the implementation stage during which the main activity of the process of programming takes place. Therefore, we can suspect that the first stage is one of the reasons why the usefulness of the system was rated negatively. Maybe feedback of this coaching stage was not sufficient enough because it could not elicit information (e.g, nouns which can be used to represent a parameter position of a predicate) hidden in the problem statement as we discussed in Section 3.4.2.

Third, the quality of feedback also plays an important role for the usefulness of the system. A clear positive attitude of the participants with respect to the comprehensiveness of feedback could not be determined (cf. Figure 5.1). One participant commented that system's feedback was of little use if it only explained the error without giving a recommendation how to correct a solution. Indeed, we intended to formulate feedback messages on the high level of programming knowledge (cf. Section 3.9) and assumed that the students are able to derive a corrective action from the feedback message. To find out which feedback messages were not useful we analysed the logged data. We sort the errors according to the levels of the structural hierarchy of a predicate.

Table 5.10: Percentage of not fixed errors

Hierarchy level	Error	Seen	Not fixed
Clause	29	18	10 (55.6%)
Subgoal	473	150	60 (40%)
Argument	899	189	64 (33.9%)
Multiplication terms	38	13	5 (38.5%)
Product factor	216	61	19 (31.1%)

5.3. LEARNING EFFECT

The second and the third column of Table 5.10 show the number of errors which have been made and whose feedback messages have been read by the participants, respectively. The last column indicates the proportion of not fixed errors, i.e., after seeing the feedback message the error was still not removed on the next solution attempt. The table indicates that feedback messages which indicate errors on the clause level were most ineffective (55.6%). This class of feedback messages might be one of the reasons which decreases the usefulness of feedback although the precision of error location was rated positively.

Chapter 6

Conclusions

6.1 Summary

Constraint-based modelling is a relative new and promising approach to domain and student modelling in tutoring systems. Instead of capturing the solution process as an admissible sequence of problem solving steps, the constraint-based approach specifies the properties which a correct solution should have. This approach has been proven successful in diagnosing errors in German utterances and in building a tutoring system for SQL. The goal of this thesis was to investigate the applicability of this approach to develop tutoring systems in the domain of programming where logic programming is focused.

As a tutoring model this thesis proposed a two-stage coaching strategy: analysing the task first, and then implementing a solution. During the first stage, the system requests the student to analyse the given task and to transform the analysis result into an adequate signature for the predicate to be implemented. If the signature is not yet appropriate, the system provides feedback and suggests the student to exhaust the information given in the problem statement. This analysis stage not only encourages students to practice the analysis of programming tasks, but also provides valuable information about the student's intention, i.e., the number and the meaning of arguments, which helps to make the subsequent diagnosis of the implementation more accurate.

To be able to coach students on both stages, we need to provide helpful feedback about the shortcomings in their solutions. For a programming problem, the solution space can be very large: a problem can be solved by applying alternative solution strategies, and each of them can be implemented in different ways. However, the traditional constraint-based approach is not able to evaluate hypotheses about the student's solution variant with respect to their plausibility. Thus, this thesis adopted a soft computing approach for solving constraint satisfaction problems to enhance the diagnostic capability for constraint-based tutoring systems. The main claim of the thesis was that constraints could be enriched with a heuristic component to evaluate the plausibility of hypotheses: constraint weights.

To model the solution space for a logic programming problem, the following techniques have been deployed: weighted constraints, semantic tables, and transformation rules. The semantic table is specified to represent semantic requirements to solve a given problem. Weighted constraints are used to model general principles of the domain and to establish a mapping between the student solution and the requirements of the semantic table.

To coach students during the first stage, weighted constraints and a signature table (an instance of the semantic table) have been used to model a space of predicate signatures which are required to diagnose shortcomings in the predicate signature specified by the student.

To model the space of implementations for the second coaching stage, in addition to weighted constraints and the implementation table (an instance of the semantic table), transformation rules have been exploited to generate possible implementation variants of an arithmetic expression (if an arithmetic expression is required) and to cover implementations using helper predicates. Together the implementation table, constraints and transformation rules span a fairly large space of implementation variants for a programming problem.

An error diagnosis algorithm has been developed on the basis of the proposed modelling techniques and makes use of constraint weights. In principle, diagnosis is carried out as an interaction of hypothesis generation and hypothesis evaluation. Hypotheses are interpretation variants for the student solution. They are generated by iteratively mapping semantic components of the student solution to the ones in the semantic table on all levels of the structural hierarchy of a solution. Each hypothesis is evaluated based on the relevant constraints. The plausibility of each hypothesis is computed by multiplying the weight value of all violated constraints into an overall score for the particular mapping. That score is used to decide on the most plausible interpretation.

To investigate the capability of weighted constraints and the usefulness of the proposed two-stage tutoring model, a tutoring system for logic programming has been implemented and two evaluation studies have been conducted. In the first study, the system has been evaluated with respect to its diagnostic capability. The evaluation study showed that the system was able to hypothesize the strategy in 90.8% of the student implementations and to diagnose errors correctly in 92.7% of the cases, in which the strategy was correctly identified. In comparison to other existing tutoring systems for programming, the diagnostic accuracy of the system implemented for this thesis (INCOM) is competitive, and thus the proposed Hypothesis 1 and

6.1. SUMMARY

2 have been confirmed:

- **Hypothesis 1**: *It is possible to build a domain model that covers a large solution space for a logic programming problem using the representation of weighted constraints and semantic tables, and a set of transformation rules.*

- **Hypothesis 2**: *Using the representations defined in Hypothesis 1, it is possible to develop an algorithm to diagnose errors in a logic program and to hypothesize the strategy underlying a solution correctly.*

The primary use of constraint weights was to control the process of error diagnosis. During this process, the interaction between hypothesis generation and hypothesis evaluation makes use of constraint weights to decide on the most plausible hypothesis about the solution strategy pursued by the student. In addition, weight values of the violated constraints have been used to determine the order in which feedback messages are presented to the student. Thus, **Hypothesis 3** can be considered true: *Using constraint weights, it is possible to prioritize feedback according to the importance of error.*

In the course of modelling the solution space for logic programming problems, weighted constraints were an effective means to model general domain principles which are not specific to a programming problem. Since standard solution strategies, which are conceived of as patterns, can be applied to solve a certain class of problems and are also not specific to a problem, we deployed weighted constraints to model standard solution strategies. Therefore, **Hypothesis 4** can also be considered true: *It is possible to create a knowledge base of standard solution strategies in logic programming using weighted constraints and to group feedback messages in a coherent manner.*

The second evaluation study has been conducted to investigate the learning effectiveness contributed by the system INCOM. The evaluation study showed that the students of the experimental group who used the system made significant learning gains and outperformed the control group by between 0.23 and 0.33 standard deviations. This indicates that the system had a small effect on the process of improving the programming skills of students. In addition, when evaluating the students' attitudes, we noticed that most students agree that the system provides precise error locations, that they are motivated by the system, and that they are confident to be able to solve programming problems of the same type. Therefore, **Hypothesis 5** has been confirmed: *A tutoring system for logic programming, which is developed on the basis of weighted constraints, semantic tables, a set of transformation rules, and the two-stage coaching model, is able to help students improve their skills in solving logic programming problems.*

Although the weighted constraint-based error diagnosis approach proposed in this work has shown encouraging results, it has some limitations. First, it is not possible to diagnose arbitrary helper predicates defined by the student because we are not able to anticipate all possible helper predicates the student intends to use. Currently, we are only able to handle two cases of helper predicates: accumulative predicates and helper predicates used to extract a part of code from its main predicate. For the first case, we anticipate the implementation of the accumulative predicate by specifying appropriate components in the semantic table. For the second one, we apply the folding/unfolding transformation techniques to embed the code of the helper predicate into its main predicate. However, these techniques can only be applied if not both the helper predicate and the main one implement a recursion.

The second limitation of the approach proposed in this thesis is that the semantic table covers only possible solution strategies which can be anticipated by the problem author. If the student develops a new solution strategy which has not been specified in the semantic table, the system matches the student implementation to the most likely generalised solution description, and the resulting feedback will not be in accordance with the intention of the student.

With respect to the coaching strategy, the two-stage coaching model did not receive a high acceptance from the participants of the evaluation study. This might be explained by two reasons. First, students were not familiar with the requirement that a programming task needs be analysed prior to the implementation. Second, the coaching during the task analysis was not effective to help students understand the problem. Students were required to identify information and goals given in a problem statement. However, some information (e.g., the data type for an argument position) could not always be identified directly from the problem statement and the coaching strategy has no means to help students reason about such information. As a consequence, participants of the experimental group needed a lot of time for the task analysis stage: they spent almost 32.5% of total experiment time (60 minutes) to analyse five programming tasks.

6.2 Thesis Contributions

This dissertation builds on previous research on cognitive modelling approaches, intelligent tutoring systems for programming, techniques of program analysis, and constraints satisfaction problems. It is novel in several ways:

Contribution #1: This thesis applied the constraint-based modelling approach (Ohlsson, 1996) to model the solution space for a programming problem. In addition, this thesis adopted the idea of the probabilistic approach to solving constraint satisfaction problems to enhance

6.2. THESIS CONTRIBUTIONS

the error diagnosis capability of constraint-based tutoring systems. That is, each constraint is associated with a heuristic value - a constraint weight. *In this thesis, the strengths and weaknesses of the weighted constraint-based approach have been investigated to develop tutoring systems in the domain of logic programming.* Constraint weights served three purposes: 1) controlling the process of error diagnosis, 2) hypothesising the strategy underlying the solution correctly, and 3) ranking feedback messages according to the severity of diagnosed errors.

In the course of checking the semantic correctness of the student solution, weighted constraints not only were used to check the structure of the solution, but also served to model the sequential order of programming constructs, e.g., the sequential order of two subgoals. Furthermore, weighted constraints can be used to check the state of variables (in logic programming, the state of a variable can be either *instantiated* or *free*). Thus, a small aspect of procedural programming had been modelled using weighted constraints. Whether this approach can be applied to the domain of state-dependent programming languages, remains open.

Contribution #2: *With respect to presenting feedback, this thesis has introduced the necessary means to prioritize feedback.* An additional benefit of using weighted constraints is that errors which are derived from violated constraints can be distinguished according to their severity because each constraint is attached with a constraint weight indicating its importance. Thus, feedback messages can be ranked according to importance. In traditional constraint-based tutoring systems, such an ability is not available. Model tracing tutors, for instance, present feedback in the order in which the problem solving steps have been specified in the model.

Contribution #3: *In terms of grouping diagnostic results, this thesis adopted the concept of patterns to describe standard solution strategies in the domain of logic programming.* Again, weighted constraints were used to model patterns. Errors which were derived from constraint violations of the same pattern can be grouped together, and feedback messages can be presented in a coherent manner. This way, students are motivated to focus on the solution strategy being implemented. None of the existing tutoring systems for programming which have been reviewed in Section 2.5 has addressed this issue so far.

Contribution #4: *The representation of the semantic table can also be considered a contribution of this thesis* because it implements two new ideas. First, the semantic table is used to represent alternative solution strategies of implementation for a given programming problem, instead of using a single expert model or a single ideal solution like in other existing constraint-based tutoring systems. Second, semantic requirements are represented by generalised model solutions. Thus, different implementation variants are covered. In addition, separating the representation of semantic requirements from constraints has the advantage that constraints become problem-independent and need not to be re-specified if new problems are added.

Contribution #5: *With respect to modelling a tutoring strategy for tutoring systems in the domain of programming, this thesis has introduced a two-stage coaching model which requires students to analyse the programming task prior to the implementation.* The separation of coaching during the phase of *task analysis* from the phase of *implementation* has not been addressed (or very little) by existing tutoring systems for programming so far (Note that, only systems, which have been evaluated with respect to learning benefits, are considered).

6.3 Future Research

Research question #1: In this thesis, it has been shown that the system INCOM, which has been built using weighted constraints, semantic tables, and transformation rules, and applying the proposed two-stage coaching model, was able to help students improve their programming skills in logic programming. However, feedback quality needs to be improved. Especially, error diagnoses concerning the existence of co-references should be able to explain why such components are required. In the example of diagnosing errors in the student implementation demonstrated in Section 3.8.4, the system generated Hint 2, which indicates that the student has missed a co-reference between two positions B and C, and Hint 3 which shows the co-reference between two positions A and B is superfluous (Figure 6.1).

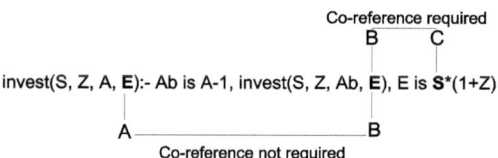

Figure 6.1: Compressible diagnostic results

Menzel (1992) suggested compressing diagnostic results by combining appropriate diagnostic results to generate corrective hints that show what kind of action the student has to carry out to improve her solution. For example, since changing a variable in the clause head is less likely than in the body, Hint 2 and Hint 3 can be combined into a corrective hint: *Change the variable at position B*. Such a corrective hint shows the student what she has to do. Which kind of diagnostic results can be compressed to generate corrective hints, is a question for further research.

The approach of compressing diagnostic results has the advantage that its feedback message provides a clear guidance which action needs to be performed. However, this kind of information

6.3. FUTURE RESEARCH

does not explain *why* this action is necessary or why those components (e.g., co-references) are required or not. Since semantic constraints are used to compare the existence of components of a generalised solution description with the student solution, feedback messages about the existence of required components can be derived; no further information about the reason of the existence of such a component is available. To enhance feedback messages with such information it would be necessary to include an explanation about the necessity of each component into the semantic table. Alternatively, a mechanism to infer this kind of information from constraint violations might be devised. For example, the corrective hint above can be extended to: *Change the variable at the position B to establish the co-reference between the positions B and C because the total investment is calculated by summing the interest of the decremented period and the current amount of money.*

Research question #2: In Section 3.5.1 we discussed two approaches to model properties of correct solutions for a problem: using either constraints or a higher abstraction of correct solutions. We chose the latter approach and proposed the concept of a semantic table, because it makes the authoring process easier and the constraint specification is simpler than the former approach. We also might think about a compromise approach: i.e., the author may provide abstractions of correct solutions while the system tries to infer problem-specific constraints from them. Constraints which share their commonalty among different solution strategies can be merged. For example, both the tail recursive and the recursive arithmetic_before strategy which are used to solve the problem *Investment* (cf. Table 1.1) require that the investment period is decremented recursively. A constraint representing this requirement can be shared across these two solution strategies. If a student implemented the decrement of investment period wrongly, this constraint would be violated and an additional feedback, for instance, *"The investment period needs to be decremented recursively"* could be provided to the student. With respect to resource consumption, this compromise approach would need more time to infer problem-specific constraints from semantic table and to check their consistency. But, could the constraints which share their commonalty across solution strategies be exploited to enhance feedback? This needs to be investigated.

Research question #3: In the previous chapter we have presented two evaluation studies which concern the diagnostic quality of a weighted constraint-based tutoring system for logic programming and the effectiveness of using diagnostic information for tutoring purposes. The results of the studies convince us that using *weighted constraints together with a semantic table and transformation rules*, we are able to model a large space of solutions for logic programming problems, and the tutoring system built on the basis of these modelling techniques can contribute to enhanced programming skills in logic programming. Can this technology also be applied to other programming paradigms, for instance, functional or imperative programming languages? This is a motivation for further research. We believe that it is possible to transfer this kind of technology to functional programming languages because they are also instances of the declarative programming paradigm. This characteristic, the atemporal nature, of declarative programming languages makes possible to formulate and to check the well-formedness conditions for a program in a static manner.

Considering imperative programming languages, the application of the weighted constraint-based model can be limited. In principle, the space of solutions can be modelled applying weighted constraints, the semantic table and transformation rules, and the semantic correctness of a solution can be checked on the basis of its structure. In addition, the requirements for ordering programming constructs, which is an important characteristic of the imperative programming paradigm, can be specified in the semantic table. However, checking the correctness of an imperative program in this way is not sufficient. The most crucial difference between the logic programming paradigm and the imperative one is that programming languages of the latter class are state-dependent, i.e., the behaviour of the program depends on the history which lead to the current state. This cannot be read off from the program text alone. For the system INCOM, we did consider the instantiation state of each variable. We derived the instantiation state of an argument from a specified predicate signature, which determines the calling mode of each argument position, and the instantiation state of all arguments is propagated through the clause from left to right. Note, in logic programming, the instantiation state of an argument can be changed from *free* to *instantiated*, and once the argument is *instantiated*, its state cannot be changed. In an imperative implementation, however, the state of variables can be changed dynamically and the instantiation state not only can be either *free* to *instantiated*, but also includes the actual value. How the weighted constraint-based model can be combined with other techniques, for instance, machine learning or collaborative learning techniques, to develop tutoring systems for imperative programming, this deserves further investigation.

Research question #4: We have applied weighted constraints in the domain of logic programming which has a large solution space but solutions can be verified by means of a test bed. The application of weighted constraints may also be promising when not only the solutions can be verified as being correct, but solutions should also be considered acceptable with respect to aesthetics and individual preferences. For instance, appealing programs and a program layout helpful for understanding (e.g., indentation rules) are preferred. These characteristics introduce aspects of ill-definedness into programming tasks (Lynch et al., 2009). Here, constraint weights could also be useful. The scale of acceptability could be measured by the total weight value of violated constraints which represent aesthetic criteria. A general question, how the aesthetic

6.3. FUTURE RESEARCH

criteria should be modelled using weighted constraints, needs to be answered in future research work.

Future Work: Although the system INCOM has demonstrated its effectiveness in helping students improve their skills in logic programming, the system needs to be improved further. First, the two-stage coaching strategy should be more flexible to allow the student to submit an incomplete/inappropriate predicate signature and the student should have the possibility to revise the predicate signature iteratively. This improvement is necessary because during the stage of task analysis the student is required to take an initial decision (e.g, choosing argument positions, data type and calling modes) and taking such a decision on an abstract level without having the possibility to use concrete programming constructs could be difficult for beginners. The second aspect of the system which should be improved is the coaching strategy on task analysis. It should be able to provide hints to help students elicit information (e.g., representing argument position or its data type) hidden in the problem statement instead of requesting the exercise author to express all information explicitly, because deriving an argument position and determining its data type are important learning goals.

Appendix A

Test A

A.1 Original Version

Aufgabe 1: Unifizieren Sie die folgenden Ausdrücke und geben Sie für den Fall, dass die Unifikation erfolgreich ist, die dabei erzeugten Variablenbindungen an.

```
groesser(F,blau)      groesser(super,T)
r(Q,f(t,b),Q)         r(d(t),f(H,b),d(H,b))
p([T|T],T,[Q|R])      p([[f,g],f,g],D,D)
```

1+1+1=3 Punkte

Aufgabe 2:

Gegeben sei die Liste der Zuschauerzahlen eines Tages für eine Reihe von Fernsehprogrammen. Für jede Sendung enthält die Liste eine Teilliste mit den Angaben zu Sender, Titel der Sendung und Zuschauerzahl (in Tausend), wobei die Eintragungen zu den Sendungen nach *fallender Zuschauerzahl sortiert sind*. Die Gesamtliste sei als Argument des einstelligen Prädikats *zuschauer1* in der Datenbasis des Prolog-Systems abgespeichert:

```
zuschauer(
  [[ard,goldmelodie,5300],
  [rtl,blutrausch,4200],
  [sat1,ran_an_die_bouletten,3500],
  [ottifanten_kanal,greif_den_zaster,3300],
  ...
  [arte,spannende_wissenschaft,3]]).
```

1. Definieren Sie ein **rekursives Prädikat**, das aus einer gegebenen Liste mit Zuschauer-Zahlen eine neue Liste berechnet, die die N meistgesehenen Sendungen des Tages enthält.

APPENDIX A. TEST A

In der erzeugten Liste soll jede Sendung wiederum durch eine dreielementige Teilliste aus Sender, Titel und Zuschauerzahl beschrieben sein. Beachten Sie insbesondere den Fall, bei dem N größer ist als die Länge der gegebenen Liste.

2. Definieren Sie ein **rekursives Prädikat**, das aus der gegebenen Gesamtliste mit Zuschauer-Zahlen eine neue Liste berechnet, die nur die Angaben für die Sendungen eines bestimmten, aber frei wählbaren Senders enthält. Die ursprüngliche Sortierreihenfolge soll bei der Berechnung nicht verändert werden.

Hinweis: Der Operator zur Negation einer Unifikation ist: Term1 \= Term2. Bitte benutzen Sie keine Systemprädikate, keinen Cut (!), und keinen Disjunktionsoperator (;)

2+4=6 Punkte

A.2 English Version

Exercise 1: Unify the following expressions. In the positive case, please show the unified values of the variables.

```
groesser(F,blau)      groesser(super,T)
r(Q,f(t,b),Q)         r(d(t),f(H,b),d(H,b))
p([T|T],T,[Q|R])      p([[f,g],f,g],D,D)
```

1+1+1=3 Points

Exercise 2:

A list represents the size of the audience for a series of TV programs. Each list element is a sublist with information about the TV station, the program title and the size of the audience (in Tsd). The list is *ordered in descending order according to the size of the audience* and is implemented as an argument of the predicate *audience/1* in the database of the Prolog system: audience([[TV1, Pro1, 5300], [TV2, Pro2, 4200],...,[TVn, ProN, 3000]]).

```
audience(
  [[ard,goldmelodie,5300],
   [rtl,blutrausch,4200],
   [sat1,ran_an_die_bouletten,3500],
   [ottifanten_kanal,greif_den_zaster,3300],
   ...
   [arte,spannende_wissenschaft,3]]).
```

1. Please define a **recursive predicate** which builds a new list containing the N most popular programs of the day. In the new list, each program should be described as a

three-element-list of a TV station, program title and the size of the audience. Consider also the case when N is greater than the length of the given list.

2. Please, define a **recursive predicate** which builds a new list of programs for a given TV station. The original order of the list should be kept.

Note: The operator for negating a unification is Term1 \= Term2. Please do not use system predicates, a Cut (!), or the disjunction operator (;). 2+4=6 Points

Appendix B

Tutorial

B.1 Original Version

Die Lösung einer Programmieraufgabe mit dem Lernsystem erfolgt in zwei Phasen: Prädikatsdeklaration und Prädikatsdefinition. In der ersten Phase sollen Sie die Aufgabenstellung analysieren und die benötigten Argumentpositionen, Argumenttypen und Argumentmodi identifizieren. Abbildung B.1 zeigt Ihnen die notwendigen Schritte. Wenn Sie Schwierigkeiten mit der Benutzungsschnittstelle für die Prädikats-Deklaration haben, können Sie unter **Prädikats-Deklaration: Hinweis** Erläuterungen zu den Arbeitsschritten dieser Phase finden.

In der zweiten Phase haben Sie die Möglichkeit, die Prädikatsdefinition selbst einzugeben. In dieser Phase soll Ihnen das System helfen, ein Prädikat zu definieren, das den Anforderungen der Aufgabenstellung und den Festlegungen der Prädikats-deklaration entspricht. Abbildung B.2 zeigt Ihnen die notwendigen Schritte. Wenn Sie Schwierigkeiten mit der Benutzungsschnittstelle für die Prädikats-Definition haben, können Sie unter **Prädikats-Definition: Hinweis** Erläuterungen zu den Arbeitsschritten dieser Phase finden. Bitte beachten Sie auf folgende Hinweise: 1) Bitte benutzen Sie keine History-Elemente des Browsers: Nach-vorne, Zurück, und Abbrechen; 2) Bitte benutzen Sie keine Systemprädikate, keinen Cut (!), und keinen Disjunktionsoperator (;).

B.2 English Version

The system INCOM requires you to go through two phases in order to be able to solve a programming problem successfully: specifying a predicate signature and implementing a predicate. During the first phase, you should analyse the description of the given problem task. That is, you have to identify the required number of argument positions, and to specify the data structure, and the calling mode for the identified argument positions. Figure B.1 shows

B.2. ENGLISH VERSION

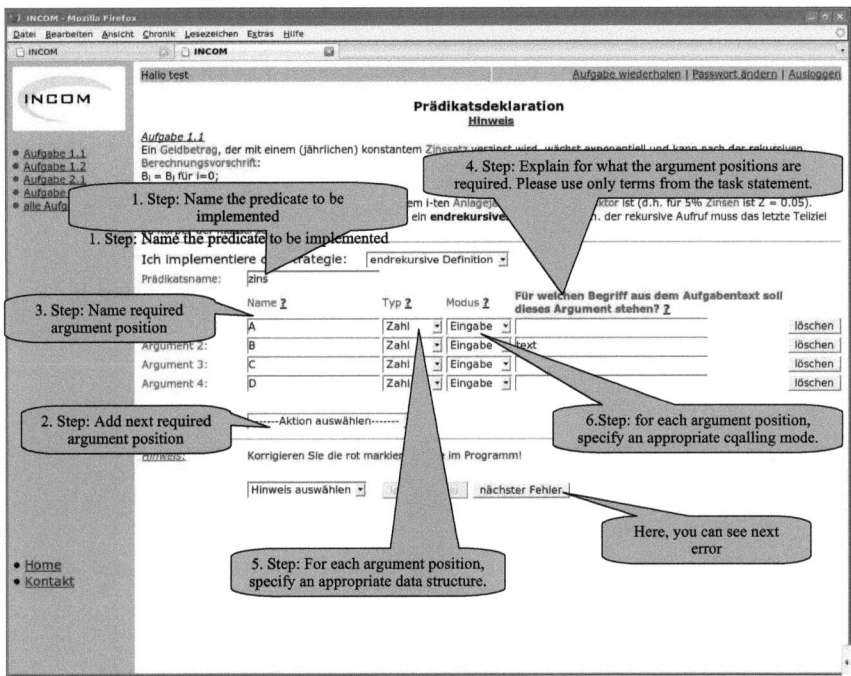

Figure B.1: A tutorial for the first coaching stage: task analysis

the steps required to specify a predicate signature. If you have any difficulty, you can find further information by clicking on the link **Prädikatsdeklaration: Hinweis**.

During the second phase, you have the possibility to input your predicate definition. The system attempts to help you to define a predicate which satisfies the requirements in the problem description and corresponds to the predicate signature you have specified. Figure B.2 shows the necessary steps. If you have any difficulty with the user interface of this phase, you can look for help by clicking on the link **Prädikatsdefinition: Hinweis**. Please consider the following remarks while using the system: 1) Do not use the History buttons of the browser: Go-forward, Go-back, and Stop; 2) Do neither use system predicates which are not listed, nor the Cut (!) or the disjunction operator (;).

APPENDIX B. TUTORIAL

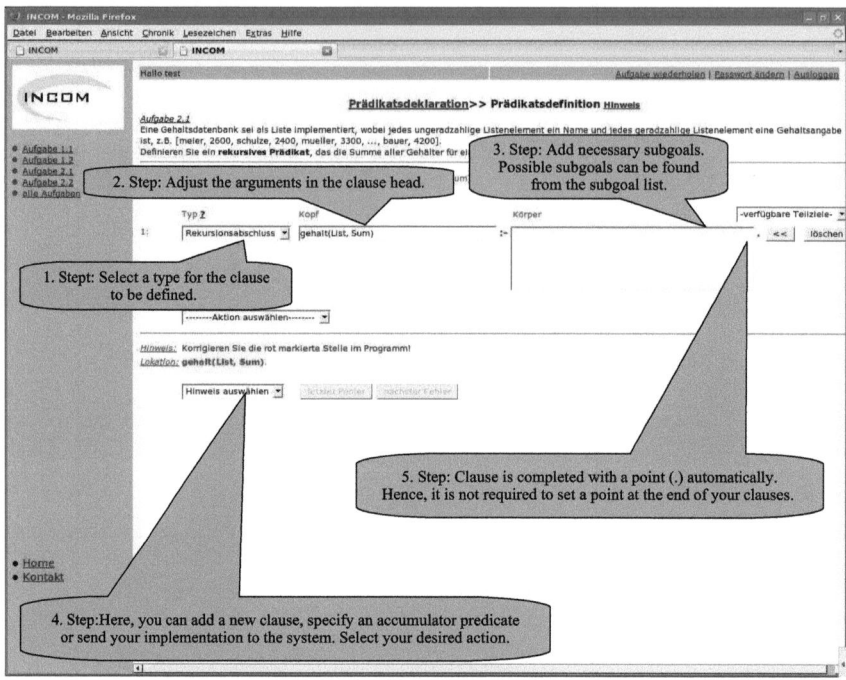

Figure B.2: A tutorial for the second coaching stage: implementation.

Appendix C

Experiment Exercises

C.1 Original Version

Aufgabe 1: (maximale Bearbeitungsdauer 35 Minuten)
Ein Geldbetrag, der mit einem (jährlichen) konstantem Zinssatz verzinst wird, wächst exponentiell und kann nach der rekursiven Berechnungsvorschrift:
$B_i = B_i$ für i=0;
$B_i = (1+Z)*B_{i-1}$ sonst,
ermittelt werden, wobei B_i das Endguthaben nach dem i-ten Anlagejahr und Z der Zinsfaktor ist (d.h. für 5% Zinsen ist Z = 0.05).

1. Bilden Sie die angegebene Berechnungsvorschrift in ein **rekursives** Prolog-Prädikat ab.
2. Definieren Sie ein **nichtrekursives** Prädikat mit der gleichen Signatur wie in Aufgabenteil 1.
3. Wandeln Sie Ihre Lösung für Aufgabenteil 1 in ein **endrekursives** Prädikat um, d.h. der rekursive Aufruf muss das letzte Teilziel im Körper der Klausel sein.

Aufgabe 2: (maximale Bearbeitungsdauer 25 Minuten)
Ein Produktverzeichnis sei als Liste implementiert, wobei jedes ungeradzahlige Listen-element eine Produktbezeichnung und jedes geradzahlige Listenelement eine Wert-angabe in Euro ist, z.B. [bett, 1600, schrank, 900, sofa, 3300, ..., schlafzimmer, 4200].

- Definieren Sie ein Prädikat, das den aktuellen Wert des Produktbestandes berechnet.
- Definieren Sie ein Prädikat, mit dem für die gegebene Produktliste beliebiger Länge eine neue Liste berechnet wird, die die folgenden Wertanpassungen berück-sichtigt:
    1. der Wert aller Produkte bis einschließlich 3000 Euro wird um 3% erhöht;
    2. der Wert alle Produkte oberhalb von 3000 Euro wird um 2% erhöht.

Hinweis: Die Darstellung für 3% und 2% entspricht 0.03 und 0.02 in Prolog.

C.2 English Version

Exercise 1: (Time limit: 35 minutes)

The return of investing an amount of money at a constant yearly interest rate can be computed according to the following recursive rule:

$B_i = B_i$ for i=0;

$B_i = (1+Z)*B_{i-1}$ otherwise,

where B_i represents the return of an investment period of i years, and Z is the yearly interest rate (e.g., for 5% interest rate, $Z = 0.05$).

1. Please map the given recursive rule to a **recursive** Prolog predicate.
2. Please define a **non-recursive** predicate with the same signature as in Assignment 1.
3. Please convert your solution for Assignment 1 into a **tail recursive** predicate, i.e., the recursive subgoal must be the last one in a clause body.

Exercise 2: (Time limit: 25 minutes)

A product database is implemented as a list whose odd elements represent names and even elements represent a price in Euro. For example: `[bed, 1600, cupboard, 900, sofa, 3300, ..., sleeping room, 4200]`.

- Define a predicate which calculates the current value of the product inventory.
- Define a predicate which creates a new product list according to the following rules:
    1. Value of products less or equal 3000 Euro will be raised 3%
    2. Value of products above 3000 Euro will be raised 2%

    Notice: the representation of 3% and 2% corresponds to 0.03 and 0.02 in Prolog, respectively.

Appendix D

Test B

D.1 Original Version

Aufgabe 1: Unifizieren Sie die folgenden Ausdrücke und geben Sie für den Fall, dass die Unifikation erfolgreich ist, die dabei erzeugten Variablenbindungen an.

```
        alter(hans,E)         alter(F, klein)
           t(x,y,y)              t(A,B,A)
p([[[m], m], m, [m]], [m])   p([[A|B]|C], A)
```

1+1+1=3 Punkte

Aufgabe 2: Der Bestand an Kraftfahrzeugen einer Firma sei als Liste von zwei-elementigen Listen gegeben, wobei das erste Element einer Unterliste das polizeiliche Kennzeichen und das zweite das Baujahr angibt, z.B.

```
[[hh-gu_12-67, 2002],
 [hh-wa_34-25, 1999],
 ..., [hh-ba_39-29, 2003]]
```

Die Leitung des Unternehmens benötigt einen überblick über die Altersstruktur der vorhandenen Fahrzeuge und bittet Sie um verschiedene Informationen. Definieren Sie geeignete **rekursive Prädikate** um den jeweiligen Informationsbedarf zu befriedigen. Hinweis: Bitte benutzen Sie keine Hilfsprädikate.

1. Wieviele Kraftfahrzeuge sind derzeit im Bestand? (2 Punkte)
2. Welche Fahrzeuge sind älter als 5 Jahre? (Das aktuelle Jahr ist 2009) (4 Punkte)

2+4=6 Punkte

D.2 English version

Exercise 1: Unify the following expressions. In the positive case, please show the unified values of the variables.

                alter(hans,E)   alter(F, klein)

                    t(x,y,y)   t(A,B,A)

     p([[[m], m], m, [m]], [m])   p([[A|B]|C], A)

1+1+1=3 Points

Exercise 2: The car store of a company is implemented as a list of two-element lists, where the first and the second element represent the licence number and the year of construction of each car, respectively. For example,

[[hh-gu_12-67, 2002],

[hh-wa_34-25, 1999],

..., [hh-ba_39-29, 2003]]

The management of the company needs an overview of the age structure of the existing cars and ask you for information. You are requested to define appropriate **recursive predicates** to deliver the required information. Note: Please do not use any helper predicate.

1. How many cars are there in the current inventory? (2 Points)
2. Which cars are older than 5 years? (The current year is 2009) (4 Points)

2+4=6 Points

Appendix E

Questionnaire

E.1 Original version

Sie haben an einer Übungssitzung mit dem System INCOM teilgenommen. Bitte geben Sie uns Ihre Einschätzung. Dabei bedeutet 1 Stern "Sehr schlecht" und 5 Sterne "Sehr gut". Vielen Dank.

- Besuch der Vorlesung "Logikprogrammierung" im Semester: WS_____.
- Als wie schwer empfanden Sie die Aufgaben der Übungssitzung? (1: sehr schwer, 5: sehr einfach)
  1 [ ] 2 [ ] 3 [ ] 4 [ ] 5 [ ]
- Ist die Benutzerschnittstelle selbsterklärend?
  1 [ ] 2 [ ] 3 [ ] 4 [ ] 5 [ ]
- Sind die Angaben zum Ort eines Fehlers ausreichend?
  1 [ ] 2 [ ] 3 [ ] 4 [ ] 5 [ ]
- Sind die Systemhinweise (Feedback, Korrekturvorschläge) verständlich?
  1 [ ] 2 [ ] 3 [ ] 4 [ ] 5 [ ]
- Haben die Hinweise Sie motiviert, an der Lösung einer Aufgabe weiterzuarbeiten?
  1 [ ] 2 [ ] 3 [ ] 4 [ ] 5 [ ]
- Hat Ihnen die Aufteilung des Programmierprozesses in Deklarations- und Definitionsphase geholfen?
  1 [ ] 2 [ ] 3 [ ] 4 [ ] 5 [ ]
- Hat Ihnen das Lernsystem geholfen, eine Lösung für eine Aufgabe zu finden?
  1 [ ] 2 [ ] 3 [ ] 4 [ ] 5 [ ]
- Konnten Sie durch dieses System Ihre Kenntnisse in der Logikprogrammierung verbessern?

1 [ ] 2 [ ] 3 [ ] 4 [ ] 5 [ ]
- Würden Sie ein solches System zum Lösen Ihrer Hausaufgaben benutzen?
1 [ ] 2 [ ] 3 [ ] 4 [ ] 5 [ ]
- Nachdem Sie mit dem Lernsystem gearbeitet haben, würden Sie weitere Aufgaben aus der gleichen Problemklasse lösen können?
1 [ ] 2 [ ] 3 [ ] 4 [ ] 5 [ ]
- Sie können uns weitere Anregungen, Kritik und Vorschläge hier mitteilen. Wir bedanken uns dafür bei Ihnen sehr herzlich.

E.2 English version

You have participated in an experiment session using the system INCOM. Please tell us your opinion by rating between 1 star ("Very bad") and 5 stars ("very good"). Thank you.

- How difficult did you find the experiment exercises? (1: very difficult, 5: very simple)
- Is the user interface comprehensible?
- Is the error location sufficiently precise?
- Are the feedback messages comprehensible ?
- Did the system feedback motivate you to continue solving a problem?
- Did the separation of the process of programming into two the stages for specifying a signature and implementing help you?
- Did the system help you to find the predicate solution for a given problem?
- Could you improve your knowledge in logic programming?
- Would you use such a system to do your homework?
- After using this system, would you be able to solve other problem tasks of the same type?
- You can tell us your comment, critique, and suggestion here.

Appendix F

A Programming Task: Calculate salaries

A salary database is implemented as a list whose odd elements represent names and even elements represent salary in Euro. For example: [meier, 3600, schulze, 5400, mueller, 6300, ..., bauer, 4200]. Define a predicate which sums all saleries for a list of arbitrary length.

Appendix G

A Sample Student Solution

G.1 Example 1

The following student solution was intended to solve the problem Exercise 2 in Appendix A. It is uncertain whether the student intended to implement the predicate *liebsten/3* using normal recursion or using tail recursion by defining an accumulative predicate *lieb/4*. If she intended to implement the normal variant of recursion, then the recursive case of *liebsten/3* is not correct and the third clause is superfluous. If she intended to implement a tail recursion, then the first clause is superfluous, the update of the accumulator argument is not correct, and a base case for the accumulator predicate *lieb/4* is missing. Since we have to provide manually an appropriate predicate signature for each student solution in the test corpus, we are not sure which solution strategy the student implemented. Thus, we assigned this solution to the group *not understandable*.

```
% liebsten(TopN, [Zuschauer], [])
liebsten(N, [], []).
liebsten(N, [Zuschauer], Erg):-lieb(N, [Zuschauer], [], Erg).

lieb(N, [H|T], Acc, Erg):-
    N1 is N-1,
    Acc1 is [H|Acc],
    lieb(N1, T, Acc1, Erg).
```

G.2 Example 2

The following student solution for the problem task *Sum salaries* is a typical candidate of the group *not understandable* because it is implemented with many unnecessary helper predicates, e.g., *odd/1*, *even/1*, and thus, we are not able to hypothesize their purpose in the context of the solution.

```
gehalt([K|R]) :- R>0, R

gehalt1([], X,F).
gehalt1([K|R], X,F):-
    X1 is X+1,
    odd(X1), gehalt1(R,X1, F);
    X1 is X+1, even(X1), F1 is F+K,
    Gehalt1(R, X1, F1).

Gehalt(L,R):-gehalt1(L, 0,0).

Odd(X):-1 is X mod Z.
Even(X):- 0 is X mod Z.
```

Bibliography

Alexander, C. (1979). *The Timeless Way of Building*. New York: Oxford University Press.

Anderson, J. R. (1993). *Rules of the Mind*. New Jersey: Lawrence Erlbaum Associates.

Anderson, J. R., S. Betts, J. L. Ferris, and J. M. Fincham (2010). Neural imaging to track mental states while using an intelligent tutoring system. *Proceedings of the National Academy of Science 107*, 7018–7023.

Anderson, J. R., F. Conrad, A. T. Corbett, J. M. Fincham, D. Hoffman, and Q. Wu (1993). Computer programming and transfer. In J. R. Anderson (Ed.), *Rules of the mind*, pp. 205–234. Lawrence Erlbaum Associates.

Anderson, J. R., A. T. Corbett, K. R. Koedinger, and R. Pelletier (1995). Cognitive tutors: Lessons learned. *Journal of the Learning Sciences 4*, 167–207.

Anderson, J. R. and B. Reiser (1985). The Lisp tutor. *Byte 10*, 159–175.

Anderson, J. R. and E. Skwarecki (1986). The automated tutoring of introductory computer programming. *Communication ACM 29*(9), 842–849.

Bain, S., J. Thornton, and A. Sattar (2004). Methods of automatic algorithm generation. In C. Zhang, H. W. Guesgen, and W. K. Yeap (Eds.), *PRICAI 2004: Trends in Artificial Intelligence*, Volume 3157 of *Lecture Notes in Computer Science*, pp. 144–153. Springer Berlin/Heidelberg.

Beck, K., R. Crocker, G. Meszaros, J. Vlissides, J. O. Coplien, L. Dominick, and F. Paulisch (1996). Industrial experience with design patterns. In *Proceedings of the 18th international conference on Software engineering*, Washington, DC, USA, pp. 103–114. IEEE Computer Society.

Bieliková, M. and P. Návrat (1998). Learning programming in prolog using schemata. *ACM SIGPLAN Notices 33*(2), 41–47.

Bol, R. N. (1995). *Loop checking in logic programming*. Amsterdam, The Netherlands: CWI (Centre for Mathematics and Computer Science).

Bonar, J. and R. Cunningham (1988). Bridge: Tutoring the programming process. In J. Psotka, L. D. Massey, and S. A. Mutter (Eds.), *Intelligent Tutoring Systems: Lessons learned*, pp. 409–434. Hillsdale, N. J.: Lawrence Erlbaum Associates.

Bowles, A. and P. Brna (1999). Introductory Prolog: a suitable selection of programming techniques. In P. Brna, B. du Boulay, and H. Pain (Eds.), *Learning to Build and Comprehend Complex Information Structures: Prolog as a Case Study*, pp. 167–178. Ablex.

Brna, P. (1993). Teaching prolog techniques. *Computers and Education 20*(1), 111–117.

Brna, P. (2001). *Prolog Programming A First Course*. Learning Unit, University of Leeds, UK.

Brna, P., A. Bundy, T. Dodd, M. Eisenstadt, C.-K. Looi, H. Pain, D. Robertson, B. Smith, and M. V. Someren (1999). Programming techniques for Prolog. In P. Brna, B. du Boulay, and H. Pain (Eds.), *Learning to Build and Comprehend Complex Information Structures: Prolog as a Case Study*, pp. 143–166. Ablex.

Brown, J., A. Collins, and P. Duguid (1989). Situated cognition and the culture of learning. *Educational Researcher 18*(1), 32.

Brown, J. S. and K. VanLehn (1980). Repair theory: A generative theory of bugs in procedural skills. *Cognitive Science 4*, 379–426.

Collins, A., J. S. Braun, and S. E. Newman (1989). Cognitive apprenticeship: Teaching the crafts of reading, writing and mathematics. In L. B. Resnick (Ed.), *Knowing, Learning And Instruction. Essays In Honour Of Robert Glaser*, pp. 453–494. Lawrence Earlbaum Associates.

Corbett, A. T., K. R. Koedinger, and J. R. Anderson (1997). Intelligent tutoring systems. In M. G. Helander, T. K. Landauer, and P. Prabhu (Eds.), *Handbook of Human-Computer Interaction*, pp. 859–874. The Netherlands: Elsevier Science.

Deek, F. P. and J. McHugh (1999). A survey and critical review of tools for learning programming. *Journal of Computer Science Education 8*(2), 130–178.

Dewey, J. (Ed.) (1910). *How we think*. Dover Publications.

Dubois, D., H. Fargier, and H. Prade (1996). Possibility theory in constraint satisfaction problems: Handling priority, preference and uncertainty. *Applied Intelligence 6*, 287–309.

Ducassé, M. and A.-M. Emde (1988). A review of automated debugging systems: knowledge, strategies and techniques. In *Proceedings of the 10th international conference on Software engineering*, Los Alamitos, CA, USA, pp. 162–171. IEEE Computer Society Press.

Eisenstadt, M., M. Keane, and T. Rajan (Eds.) (1993). *Novice Programming Environments: explorations in human-computer interaction and artificial intelligence*. Laurence Erlbaum.

Fargier, H. and J. Lang (1993). Uncertainty in constraint satisfaction problems: a probabilistic approach. In R. K. Michael Clarke and S. Moral (Eds.), *Proceedings of the European Conference ECSQARU '93*, pp. 97–104. Springer.

Feddon, J. and N. Charness (1999). Component relationships depend on skill in programming. In *Proceedings of 11th Annual PPIG Workshop, University of Leeds, UK*.

Fleming, M. and W. Levie (1993). *Instructional message design: principles from the behavioral and cognitive sciences*. Englewood Cliffs NJ: Educational Technology Publications.

Foth, K. A. (2007). *Hybrid Methods of Natural Language Analysis*. Shaker Verlag, Germany.

Freuder, E. and R. Wallace (1992). Partial constraint satisfaction. *Artificial Intelligence 58*, 21–70.

Gamma, E., R. Helm, R. Johnson, and J. Vlissides (1995). *Design patterns: elements of reusable object-oriented software*. Addison-Wesley Professional.

Gegg-Harrison, T. S. (1993). *Exploiting program schemata in a Prolog tutoring system*. Ph. D. thesis, Department of Computer Science, Duke University.

Gegg-Harrison, T. S. (1999). Exploiting program schemata to teach recursive programming. In P. Brna, B. du Boulay, and H. Pain (Eds.), *Learning to Build and Comprehend Complex Information Structures: Prolog as a Case Study*, pp. 347–379. Ablex.

Gelder, A. V. (1989). Negation as failure using tight derivations for general logic programs. *Journal of Logic Programming 6*(1&2), 109–133.

Gick, M. L. (1986). Problem-solving strategies. *Education Psychologist 21*, 99–120.

Gutierrez-Santos, S. and M. Mavrikis (2008). Intelligent support for exploratory environments: Where are we and where do we want to go now? In M. M. Sergio Gutierrez-Santos (Ed.), *Proceedings of the 1st International Workshop on Intelligent Support for Exploratory Environments held at the EC-TEL'08 Conference*, pp. 1–10.

Guzdial, M., L. Hohmann, M. Konneman, C. Walton, and E. Soloway (1998). Supporting programming and learning-to-program with an integrated CAD and scaffolding workbench. *Interactive Learning Environments 6*(1,2), 143–179.

Haynes, S. M. (1995). Explaining recursion to the unsophisticated. *ACM SIGCSE Bulletin 27*(3), 3–6.

Heffernan, N. T., K. R. Koedinger, and L. Razzaq (2008). Expanding the model-tracing architecture: A 3rd generation intelligent tutor for algebra symbolization. *International Journal of Artificial Intelligence in Education 18*(2), 153–178.

Hietala, P. (1993). Teaching AI through Prolog programming techniques. *Computers and Education 20*(1), 133–139.

Hoc, J.-M. (1988). *Cognitive psychology of planning*. San Diego, CA, USA: Academic Press Professional.

Hong, J. (2004). Guided programming and automated error analysis in an intelligent Prolog tutor. *International Journal of Human-Computer Studies 61*(4), 505–534.

Jeffries, R., A. A. Turner, P. G. Polson, and M. E. Atwood (1981). The processes involved in designing software. *Cognitive skills and their acquisition*.

Johnson, W. L. (1990). Understanding and debugging novice programs. *Artificial Intelligence 42*(1), 51–97.

Johnson, W. L. and E. Soloway (1985). PROUST: an automatic debugger for pascal programs. *BYTE 10*(4), 179–190.

Joni, S. and E. Soloway (1986). But my program runs. Discourse rules for novice. *Programmers Journal of Educational Computing Research 2*(1), 95–125.

Kadiyala, M. and B. Crynes (1998). Where's the proof? A review of literature on effectiveness of information technology in education. In *Proceedings of the 28th Annual Frontiers in Education*, Washington, DC, USA, pp. 33–37. IEEE Computer Society.

Klemm, K. and A. Klemm (2010). Ausgaben für Nachhilfe - teurer und unfairer Ausgleich für fehlende individuelle Forderung. *Bertelsmann Stiftung*.

Kodaganallur, V., R. Weitz, and D. Rosenthal (2005). A comparison of model-tracing and constraint-based intelligent tutoring paradigms. *International Journal of Artificial Intelligence in Education 15*(2), 117–144.

Kodaganallur, V., R. Weitz, and D. Rosenthal (2006). An assessment of constraint-based tutors: A response to Mitrovic and Ohlsson's critique of "a comparison of model-tracing and constraint-based intelligent tutoring paradigms". *International Journal of Artificial Intelligence in Education 16*, 291–321.

Lane, H. C. (2004). *Natural language tutoring and the novice programmer*. Ph. D. thesis, University of Pittsburgh.

Lane, H. C. and K. VanLehn (2005). Teaching the tacit knowledge of programming to novices with natural language tutoring. *Computer Science Education, Special issue on doctoral research in CS Education 15*(3), 183–201.

Larman, C. and V. R. Basili (2003). Iterative and incremental development: A brief history. *Computer 36*(6), 47–56.

Le, N.-T. and W. Menzel (2008a). The coverage of error diagnosis in logic programming using weighted constraints - the case of an ill-defined domain. In *Proceedings of the 21st International FLAIRS Conference, Special Track on Intelligent Tutoring Systems*.

Le, N.-T. and W. Menzel (2008b). Towards an evaluation methodology of diagnostic accuracy for ill-defined domains. In *Proceedings of the 16th International Conference on Computers in Education*.

Le, N.-T., W. Menzel, and N. Pinkwart (2010). Considering ill-definedness of problems from the aspect of solution space. In *Proceedings of the 23st International FLAIRS Conference, Special Track on Intelligent Tutoring Systems*.

Legree, P., P. Gillis, and M. Orey (1993). The quantitative evaluation of intelligent tutoring systems applications: product and process criteria. *International Journal of Artificial Intelligence in Education 4*(2/3), 209–226.

Lloyd, J. W. (1987). *Foundations of logic programming*. Springer-Verlag New York.

Looi, C.-K. (1991). Automatic debugging of Prolog programs in a Prolog intelligent tutoring system. *Instructional Science 20*, 215 – 263.

Lynch, C., K. D. Ashley, N. Pinkwart, and V. Aleven (2009, August). Concepts, structures, and goals: Redefining ill-definedness. *International Journal of Artificial Intelligence in Education 19*, 253–266.

Malhotra, A., J. C. Thomas, J. M. Carroll, and L. A. Miller (1980). Cognitive processes in design. *International Journal of Man-Machine Studies 12*, 119–140.

Martin, B. (2001). *Intelligent Tutoring Systems: The Practical Implementation Of Constraint-based Modelling*. Ph. D. thesis, University of Canterbury.

McCracken, M., V. Almstrum, D. Diaz, M. Guzdial, D. Hagan, Y. B.-D. Kolikant, C. Laxer, L. Thomas, I. Utting, and T. Wilusz (2001). A multi-national, multi-institutional study of assessment of programming skills of first-year CS students. In *Working group reports from ITiCSE on innovation and technology in computer science education*, New York, NY, USA, pp. 125–180. ACM.

Menzel, W. (1988). Diagnosing grammatical faults - a deep-modelled approach. In *AIMSA*, pp. 319–326.

Menzel, W. (1992). *Modellbasierte Fehlerdiagnose in Sprachlehrsystemen*. Niemeyer.

Menzel, W. and I. Schröder (1998). Constraint-based diagnosis for intelligent language tutoring systems. In *Proceedings IT and KNOWS, XV. IFIP World Computer Congress*, Wien und Budapest, pp. 484–497.

Merrill, D. C., B. J. Reiser, M. Ranney, and J. G. Trafton (1992). Effective tutoring techniques: A comparison of human tutors and intelligent tutoring systems. *The Journal of the Learning Sciences 2*(3), 277–305.

Mitrovic, A., K. R. Koedinger, and B. Martin (2003). A comparative analysis of cognitive tutoring and constraint-based modeling. In P. Brusilovsky, A. T. Corbett, and F. de Rosis (Eds.), *Proceedings of the 9th International Conference on User Modeling*, pp. 313–322.

Mitrovic, A., B. Martin, and P. Suraweera (2007). Intelligent tutors for all: The constraint-based approach. *IEEE Intelligent Systems 22*(4), 38–45.

Mitrovic, A., M. Mayo, P. Suraweera, and B. Martin (2001). Constraint-based tutors: A success story. In *Proceedings of the 14th International conference on Industrial and engineering applications of artificial intelligence and expert systems*, London, UK, pp. 931–940. Springer-Verlag.

Mitrovic, A. and S. Ohlsson (1999). Evaluation of a constraint-based tutor for a database language. *International Journal of Artificial Intelligence in Education 10*, 238–256.

Mitrovic, A., P. Suraweera, B. Martin, and A. Weerasinghe (2004). DB-suite: Experiences with three intelligent, web-based database tutors. *Journal of Interactive Learning Research 15*(4), 409–432.

Návrat, P. and V. Rozinajová (1993). Making programming knowledge explicit. *Computers and Education 21*(4), 281–299.

Nielsen, J. (1993). *Usability Engineering*. AP Professional.

Ohlsson, S. (1994). Constraint-based student modelling. In J. E. Greer and G. I. McCalla (Eds.), *Student Modelling: The Key to Individualized Knowledge-based Instruction*, pp. 167–189. Berlin: Springer-Verlag.

Ohlsson, S. (1996). Learning from performance errors. *Psychological Review*, 241–262.

Ohlsson, S. and N. Bee (1991). Radical strategy variability: a challenge to models of procedural learning. In *Proceedings of the international conference of the learning science*, pp. 351–356.

Ohlsson, S. and A. Mitrovic (2006). Constraint-based knowledge representation for individualized instruction. *Computer Science and Information Systems 3*(1), 1–22.

Ohlsson, S. and E. Rees (1991). The function of conceptual understanding in the learning of arithmetic procedures. *Journal Cognition and Instruction 8*(2), 103–179.

Payne, S. J. and H. R. Squibb (1990). Algebra mal-rules and cognitive accounts of error. *Cognitive Science 14*(3), 445–481.

Pennington, N. (1987). Comprehension strategies in programming. In G. M. Olson, S. Sheppard, and E. Soloway (Eds.), *Emperical studies of programmers: 2nd workshop*, pp. 100–113. Ablex Corp.

Pennington, N. and B. Grabowski (1990). The tasks of programming. In J.-M. Hoc, T. R. G. Green, R. Samurcay, and D. J. Gilmore (Eds.), *Psychology of Programming*, pp. 45–62. Newyork: Academic Press Ltd.

Perkins, D. N., C. Hancock, R. Hobbs, F. Martin, and R. Simmons (1989). Conditions of learning in novice programmers. In E. Soloway and J. C. Spohrer (Eds.), *Studying the Novice Programmer*. Lawrence Erlbaum Associates.

Pintrich, P. R., C. F. Berger, and P. M. Stemmer (1987). Students' programming behaviour in a Pascal course. *Journal of Research in Science Teaching 24*(5), 451–466.

Pressey, S. L. (1927). A machine for the automatic teaching of drill material. *School and Society 25*, 549–552.

Regian, J. W. (1997). Functional area analysis of intelligent computer-assisted instruction. *Report, TAPSTEM ICAI-FAA Committee, Brooks Air Force Base, Texas*.

Reiser, B., D. Kimberg, M. Lovett, and M. Ranney (1992). Knowledge representation and explanation in GIL, an intelligent tutor for programming. In J. Larkin and R. Chaby (Eds.), *Computer Assisted Instruction and Intelligent Tutoring Systems: Shared Goals and Complementary Approaches*, pp. 111–149. Lawrence Erlbaum Associates.

Reiser, B. J., P. Friedmann, J. Gevins, D. Y. Kimberg, and M. Ranney (1988). A graphical programming language interface for an intelligent LISP tutor. In *Proceedings of the SIGCHI conference on human factors in computing systems*, pp. 39–44. ACM.

Rijsbergen, C. J. V. (1979). *Information retrieval* (2 ed.). London: Butterworths.

Rist, R. S. (1989). Schema creation in programming. *Cognitive Science 13*, 389–414.

Schiex, T., C.-T. Cedex, H. Fargier, and G. Verfaillie (1995). Valued constraint satisfaction problems: Hard and easy problems.

Self, J., L. Yr, and J. A. Self (1994). Formal approaches to student modelling. In G. McCalla and J. E. Greer (Eds.), *Student Models: The key to individual education systems*. New York: Springer Verlag.

Shazeer, N. M., M. L. Littman, and G. A. Keim (1999). Solving crossword puzzles as probabilistic constraint satisfaction. In *Proceedings of the sixteenth national conference on Artificial intelligence and the eleventh Innovative applications of artificial intelligence conference*, Menlo Park, CA, USA, pp. 156–162. American Association for Artificial Intelligence.

Shneiderman, B. (1977). Teaching programming: A spiral approach to syntax and semantics. *Computers and Education 1*, 193–197.

Shute, V. J. and J. Psotka (1996). Intelligent tutoring systems: Past, present and future. In D. Jonassen (Ed.), *Handbook of Research on Educational Communications and Technology*, pp. 570–600. Macmillan, New York.

Skinner, B. F. (1958). Teaching machines. *Science 128*, 969–977.

Sleeman, D. and J. S. Brown (1982). Introduction: Intelligent tutoring systems. In Sleeman and Brown (Eds.), *Intelligent Tutoring Systems*, pp. 1–10. New York: Academic Press.

Sollohub, C. (1991). Programming templates: Professional programmer knowledge needed by the novice. *Computer Science Education 2*(3), 255–266.

Soloway, E., K. Ehrlich, J. Bonar, and J. Greenspan (1982). What do novices know about programming. In A. Badre and B. Schneiderman (Eds.), *Directions in Human-Computer Interaction*, pp. 87–122. Ablex.

Soloway, E., E. Rubin, B. Woolf, J. Bonar, and W. Johnson (1983). MENO-II: An AI-based programming tutor. *Journal of Computer-Based Instruction 10*(1), 20–34.

Soloway, E., J. C. Spohrer, and D. Littman (1988). E unum pluribus: Generating alternative designs. In R. E. Mayer (Ed.), *Teaching and Learning Computer Programming*. Lawrence Erlbaum Associates.

Sterling, L. and E. Shapiro (1994). *The Art of Prolog*. Cambridge (MA): MIT Press.

Suppes, P., M. Jerman, and D. Brian (1968). *Computer assisted instruction: Stanford's 1965-66 arithmetic program*. New York: Academic Press.

Sweller, J. (1994). Cognitive load theory, learning difficulty, and instructional design. *Learning and Instruction 4*(4), 295–312.

Tamaki, H. and T. Sato (1984). Unfold/fold transformation of logic programs. In *Proceedings of International Conference on Logic Programming*, pp. 127–138.

VanLehn, K., C. Lynch, K. Schulze, J. A. Shapiro, R. Shelby, L. Taylor, D. Treacy, A. Weinstein, and M. Wintersgill (2005). The ANDES physics tutoring system: Lessons learned. *International Journal of Artificial Intelligence in Education 15*(3), 147–204.

VanLehn, K., S. Siler, C. Murray, T. Yamauchi, and W. B. Baggett (2003). Why do only some events cause learning during human tutoring? *Cognition and Instruction 21*(3).

Vanneste, P. (1994). *A Reverse Engineering Approach to Novice Program Analysis*. Ph. D. thesis, KU Leuven Campus Kortrijk.

VanSomeren, M. W. (1990). What's wrong? Understanding beginners' problems with Prolog. *Instructional Science 19*, 257–282.

Vasconcelos, W. W. (1995). *Extracting, Organising, Designing and Reusing Prolog Programming Techniques*. Ph. D. thesis, University of Edinburgh.

Waters, R. C. (1994). Cliché-based program editors. *ACM Transactions on Programming Languages and Systems (TOPLAS) 16*(1), 102–150.

Weber, G. and P. Brusilovsky (2001). ELM-ART: An adaptive versatile system for web-based instruction. *International Journal of Artificial Intelligence in Education 12*, 351–384.

Weber, G. and A. Möllenberg (1995). ELM programming environment: a tutoring system for Lisp beginners. In K. Wender, F. Schmalhöfer, and H.-D. Boecker (Eds.), *Cognition and computer programming*, pp. 373–408. Norwood, NJ, USA: Ablex Publishing Corp.

Weiser, M. and J. Shertz (1983). Programming problem representation in novice and expert programmers. *International Journal of Man-Machine Studies 19*, 391–398.

Wender, K. F., G. Weber, and G. Waloszek (1987). Psychological considerations for the design of tutorial systems. In *Proceedings of the Third International Conference on Artificial Intelligence and Education*.

Wenger, E. (1987). *Artificial intelligence and tutoring systems: computational and cognitive approaches to the communication of knowledge*. San Francisco, CA, USA: Morgan Kaufmann Publishers Inc.

Wolf, F. M. (1986). *Meta–Analysis: Quantitative Methods for Research Synthesis*. Sage Publications, Beverly Hills.

Woolf, B. P. (2009). *Building Intelligent Interactive Tutors*. Morgan Kaufman.

Index

(de)composition, 44

accumulative predicate, 48
ADAPT, 24, 29
adaptive computer-aided instruction, 2
additive model, 64
algebraic sign, 43
alternative sequential ordering, 47
APROPOS2, 24, 26, 102, 104
argument, 42
    calling mode, 57
    data type, 57
    meaning, 57
arithmetic test, 44, 45

back-end, 93, 95
basic programming concept, 16
Beam search technique, 77, 81
buggy rule, 7, 31

calculation, 44, 45
clause, 42
clause body, 42
clause head, 42
clause type, 59
coaching, 13
communication model, 3
computer-aided instruction, 2
constraint schema, 60, 61
constraint weight, 9, 62, 73
constraint-based model, 60

context sensitive constraint, 84

declaration constraint, 67
diagnostic accuracy, 100
diagnostic validity, 24, 102
domain model, 2

effect size Cohen's d, 108
ELM-ART, 22, 27
error diagnosis, 3, 75
    constraint-based modelling, 7, 33
    library of plans and bugs, 26
    model-tracing, 7, 30
    transformation, 28
error location, 91
expert model, 31
exponential term, 43

feedback, 88
    confirmation, 89
    corrective, 89
    diagnostic, 89
    elaborative, 89
    explanatory, 89
functor, 42

general constraint, 60, 70
general constraint evaluator, 93, 97
generalised solution description, 68, 80
GIL, 22
global mapping, 80, 82

gold standard, 102

helper predicate, 48, 74
high level programming concept, 16
Hong's tutor, 24, 28, 102, 104
hypothesis evaluation, 78, 79
hypothesis generation, 76, 78, 80
hypothesis plausibility, 64, 79

ideal solution, 35, 60
implementation, 14
implementation constraint, 69
implementation diagnosis, 80, 84
instantiation state, 70
intelligent tutoring systems, 2
intention analysis, 24, 101
Investment problem, 4, 52
iterative programming process, 14

knowledge base, 93, 97

learning effect, 106
learning gain, 107
linear programming process, 14
LISP-Tutor, 20, 31
local mapping, 80, 82

matcher, 93
matching process, 78, 80
matching rule, 77
MENO-II, 24
multiplication term, 43
multiplicative model, 64

normal form, 68

parser, 93, 96
pattern constraint, 73, 91

pre-implementation constraint, 71
precision, 103
predicate signature, 57, 65
problem type, 19
product factor, 43
production rule, 31
program analyser, 24
program validation, 14
programming knowledge, 15
programming phase, 13
programming primitive, 16
Prolog pattern
    process-all-accumulator, 50
    process-all-elements, 50, 73
    test-all-elements, 50
    test-for-existence, 50
Prolog Patterns, 50
Prolog programming technique, 49
Prolog schema, 49, 90
PROPL, 22
PROUST, 24, 26, 102, 104

recall, 103
recursion, 44
relevance part, 34

satisfaction part, 34
semantic constraint, 72
semantic constraints, 61
semantic correctness, 10
semantic table, 10, 61
    implementation table, 61, 67, 92
    signature table, 61, 66
signature diagnosis, 78
solution design, 13
solution strategy, 17, 47

SQL-Tutor, 7, 21
strategy level, 80
structural hierarchy of a predicate, 43
structural hierarchy of a signature, 65
student model, 2
subgoal, 42
syntactic reformulation, 46

tacit knowledge, 15
task analysis, 13, 57
term test, 44, 46
transformation rules, 74
tutoring model, 3
tutoring system, 3
two-stage coaching, 10, 53

unfolding/folding, 74, 92
unification, 44, 46
user interface, 93
user-defined subgoal, 44, 46

weighted constraint, 64, 69

i want morebooks!

Buy your books fast and straightforward online - at one of world's fastest growing online book stores! Environmentally sound due to Print-on-Demand technologies.

Buy your books online at
www.get-morebooks.com

Kaufen Sie Ihre Bücher schnell und unkompliziert online – auf einer der am schnellsten wachsenden Buchhandelsplattformen weltweit! Dank Print-On-Demand umwelt- und ressourcenschonend produziert.

Bücher schneller online kaufen
www.morebooks.de

 VDM Verlagsservicegesellschaft mbH
Heinrich-Böcking-Str. 6-8   Telefon: +49 681 3720 174   info@vdm-vsg.de
D - 66121 Saarbrücken   Telefax: +49 681 3720 1749   www.vdm-vsg.de

Printed by Books on Demand GmbH, Norderstedt / Germany